Ken Bates
My Chelsea Dream

Ken Bates

My Chelsea Dream

Brian Woolnough

First published in Great Britain in 1998 by
Virgin Books
an imprint of Virgin Publishing Ltd
Thames Wharf Studios
Rainville Road
London W6 9HT

A catalogue record for this book is available from the British Library.

ISBN 1 85227 737 8

Typeset by TW Typesetting, Plymouth, Devon

Printed and bound by Mackays of Chatham, PLC

Contents

'When I fight there are no rules.
It is dirty.
I see no sense in being a good loser.'
Ken Bates, 1998

1 The Last Enemy

KEN BATES WAS IN A GOOD MOOD. He felt relaxed and happy. There was even a spring in his step as he rushed down London's Park Lane towards the Dorchester Hotel. Colin Hutchinson, Chelsea Football Club's chief executive and a friend of Bates for more than nine years, was trying to keep up as the two men neared their meeting. 'Don't forget, Ken, stay calm,' pleaded Hutchinson. 'Whatever you do, don't lose your temper.'

Bates had no intention of losing his temper. He had waited a long time for this. A long time to rid himself of Matthew Harding, a long time to expose the person Bates called the 'last enemy'. Oh yes, he was looking forward to the meeting. Looking forward to telling Harding, face to face, to fuck off. One last time.

It had been planned, rehearsed even, down to the last detail. Bates had called the meeting with Harding, the chairman of Benfield Insurance Group and a Chelsea supporter, who had come into Bates's life with money and promises, but who had turned into an arch-rival, a bitter enemy. It is safe to say that, by the end, indeed at this meeting, the two men hated each other.

The battle for power at Stamford Bridge, Chelsea's home in West London, had turned into a war. And Bates, old grey beard, was not going to be beaten by some upstart, even if he was worth more than £40 million.

Bates and Hutchinson were sitting in the comfortable

downstairs bar at the Dorchester for the 11.30 a.m. meeting when Harding came bounding in. He smiled at them, ordered a drink, and the three men started chatting away about nothing in particular. Harding said that he was in a hurry because he was having lunch at the House of Lords. Bates saw his chance for the first dagger thrust. He told Harding that the lunch was nothing, just a fund-raising function attended by a number of people from all walks of life. 'That miffed Matthew a bit because he liked to think he trod the corridors of power,' says Bates.

Having started with a jab to the chest, Bates went for an immediate knockout. He put his hand into the inside pocket of his suit and pulled out a long, magnolia envelope. 'Matthew, here is a bank draft for you made out for £2.7 million. Take it. We do not owe you a penny now.' The sum owed to Harding had, in fact, been £3.2 million, but £500,000 from a different account had already been released to him.

Harding looked surprised because, he said, he had been close to organising a deal that Bates would have found acceptable. 'I have the details and papers here,' he said. 'Too late,' snapped Bates, and now there was no stopping the Chelsea chairman. 'You have buggered us about too long. We are going into the future without you.'

Bates says that it was a sweet moment for him. 'We had gone public and there was a clause in our agreement with Harding stating that he could be a member of the board if we owed him money. From that day, we did not owe him a penny.

'After handing him the banker's draft for the money we owed him I followed that up with twenty-eight days' notice to chuck him off the board. I told him that he had the right to make representations to the other directors if he felt that he should not be removed, but that he should know that the vote to kick him off was seven to nil.'

Harding was gobsmacked, according to Bates. His mouth fell open and it stayed open when Bates then added: 'Now, Matthew, do me a great pleasure, and fuck off.'

Game, set and match, as they say, to Bates, the old warrior of football who takes no prisoners when it comes to street fighting. If you take him on you know what you will get. A dirty fight. And you lose. Harding had just found out that the power of this 66-year-old man is incredible, particularly when doing battle. When it comes to Chelsea there is no one to touch him, and many have tried.

He knows everything and anything about Chelsea, the people who work there and those who try to make an uninvited entrance via the front or back door. All information leads back to Uncle Ken from those who have stayed loyal to him since all this began in 1982, when he bought the club for £1 and inherited the debts. There is no question that he saved Chelsea from folding and without this extraordinary character there would be no 'Chelsea, Chelsea' today.

From day one he had a dream to make Chelsea the biggest and best club in Britain. The grandest stadium and the most successful, powerful team. Not many believed him all those years ago. Others thought they could shatter that dream by either buying him out or de-throning him by fair means or foul. He had taken them all on and won, some by knockout, others on points. What they all did not recognise, Harding, John Duggan, Peter Middleton and others, was the sheer determination, stubbornness and firepower in Bates, now 66 years old and still going strong.

His planning for war is incredible. He leaves no detail untouched. It took him weeks to plot that final showdown with Harding.

Bates knew he had to get the money to pay off Harding. His plan began at a working breakfast with a high-ranking member of a consortium bidding for the new television contract. He asked Bates what he thought would swing the contract in their favour. Bates says, 'I told him that the clubs were going through a transitional period. The new Bosman ruling on transfers had hit them. I said that what the clubs would want from television would be £50 million on the table with an unreturnable deposit for the clubs. I told him that this was the kind of package to swing the vote.'

What that consortium member did not realise, Chelsea claim, is that a few days later Colin Hutchinson had lunch with representatives of Sky Television, always the favourites to get the contract again. Hutchinson told Sky that he had heard that another consortium were putting down £50 million with an unreturnable deposit. 'Sky said they would do the same and put down the identical offer,' Bates says proudly.

'Then I went to Rick Parry, the then chief executive of the Premier League (now with Liverpool), and asked him how the money would be distributed. He told me that it would be spread through the clubs and I asked for that in writing. He said, "No problem." '

The plot was working. Bates took the written assurance from Parry to Chelsea's bank, the Co-op, and borrowed £2 million. Then he went to Doctor Marwan, who, says Bates, is an old friend of the club. 'He is an Egyptian financier who helped us when we were fighting John Duggan over the ground all those years ago. Then, he provided a twenty-nine per cent stake, which meant we could get capital.'

Marwan was indeed a good friend to Chelsea, and particularly to Bates. This London-based son-in-law of Colonel Nasser is certainly a significant figure in the club's recent history. Bates bought Marwan's shares in SB Property Company, which owned the freehold of the stadium, and Marwan agreed to let Chelsea pay back the £2 million fee in instalments. SB Property Company had guaranteed the debts of Cabra Estates, the property development company that owned a seventy per cent stake in SB. Bates immediately launched an action claiming that this agreement amounted to an unfair prejudice against the minority shareholders – why should their assets guarantee the debts of Cabra? This move by Bates proved to be an important delaying tactic in the fight to save the club from the designs of the property men.

Marwan's generosity and support was again demonstrated immediately prior to Harding's pay-off when he telegraphed £2 million into the Chelsea account. A further £3 million was raised through an offshore investment trust based in Guernsey and operated by friends of Bates. This organisation has since become the major shareholder in Chelsea Village.

Now, with £7 million, he knew he had the funds – and the power – to get rid of Harding.

Bates adds: 'The Harding thing had become impossible. We trumped him by going public. It was a significant moment. He and his lawyer had always been messing us about. One day they would say they did want the money back, the next they would say they didn't. It was a game and I was bloody well not going to put up with it any longer. I did not want a loan to him being displayed in the balance sheet as monies payable on demand. To me it was a petty battle. I wanted to get going. I had more important things to do than muck about with an upstart like this. He had lost long before that meeting in the Dorchester, although he probably didn't realise it.'

Bates, of course, had acquired a lot more money than the amount owed to Harding. The balance was his trump card. As Harding floundered under the weight of this news, Bates delivered the final blow: 'By the way, Matthew, we have just signed Frank LeBoeuf for £2.5 million. He is a French international defender, you may have heard of him.'

Bates was enjoying himself now. The enemy, trapped and cornered, was being tortured. Bates explains, 'In the end, we never told Matthew anything that was going on with the club. If we did, it appeared in the newspapers. He could not keep a secret. So we played games with him, telling him lies and laughing when he gave his friends in the media the wrong information.'

Bates took great delight in tormenting Harding with the LeBoeuf signing because it proved to his enemy that he did not know everything that was going on inside the club. 'In fact,' boasts Bates, 'he knew very little.' The news of the LeBoeuf deal gave Bates so much satisfaction because the transfer had been signed, sealed and delivered without the media, and Harding, knowing anything about it.

I was certainly caught in the middle of the extraordinary war between Bates and Harding. I had known Bates for years, ever since he took over this famous football club in 1982. You could never call him a close friend because there is too much public fire in him, too much contempt for the media for Bates to have a warm understanding with a newspaper man. I have respect for him because, without question, there would be no

Chelsea Football Club without this extraordinary character. He saved the club from going under and then saved it from the clutches of businessmen and property developers who wanted to use the prime site for housing estates and offices. I have always admired his seemingly boundless energy for a fight. He does not like to be beaten and refuses to let anyone else have the last word. I recall a news reporter from my own *Sun* newspaper calling the Bates home late at night and waking him. Bates, then a farmer, always went to bed early and got up at 5.30 a.m. But the newsman was not to know this, and it was a legitimate inquiry. The next day, Bates got up an hour early, at 4.30 a.m., and rang my own home, waking wife, children, cats, dogs, the lot. 'If I am woken, Brian Woolnough is going to be woken,' he snarled into my wife's ear, who had picked up the phone by our bed. She was, as you can imagine, not best pleased.

That, however, is typical Bates. A street fighter in every sense. But there is a warm, kind side of Bates, of course, and I have grown to know it. You will never see it in public, however, although the people who know him well describe Bates as a good friend, a kind and generous host and someone who looks after his own.

Harding was a different character altogether. Outwardly bouncy and popular, here was a man who had the potential to lower the drawbridge of hate at Chelsea and welcome in a new era. While Bates only talked in public when challenged, Harding offered up interviews, comment and lunch parties at the drop of a telephone call. I grew to like him and, yes, we became friends. He would often call and demand a meeting for a chat and a few beers and he seemed to like nothing better than the company of journalists. He was unlike Bates in almost every way.

Bates, of course, has no doubts: 'You were all taken in. The crap he gave out was often the stuff we told him because we wanted him to make a fool of himself. It appeared in the papers, just as we knew it would. He was being devious, but I knew everything that was going on, every trick he tried to play.

'If you are going to organise a coup you have to keep your

mouth shut. He couldn't do that. He would simply boast to others what he was doing. Well, what he did not realise was that I had more friends than he did. People came and told me what was happening. He made too many mistakes in his bid to get rid of me.

'After that meeting at the Dorchester the fight was virtually over, even if he would never admit it in public.

'I thought, however, that had we actually thrown him off the board he would have committed suicide because he could never have lived with that indignity.

'He would certainly have started bellyaching around and I did not need that. So we kept him, on my terms this time. He stayed as vice chairman. But it was like being Vice President of the United States – you are there in name only and you make no decisions. He stayed on my rules.'

You can feel the bitterness, can't you? The depth of hate in Bates, and there is no question that the feeling inside Harding was the same. There is also no doubt in my mind that Bates is pleased that Harding is no longer with us – not that he is dead especially, but certainly that he is no longer around to challenge him, to annoy him, to take up so much of his time.

Harding was the last enemy for Bates. It was also the most bitter of his battles because it was personal. This book plots how Bates took control of Chelsea in 1982 and fought long and hard to turn it into the multi-million pound institution it is today. From a run-down, sad giant at the start of the eighties, to a club with a magnificent stadium and a multi-national, multi-talented team today. Sixteen years. It doesn't sound like a long time, does it? – but it has often felt like a lifetime to Bates.

Nothing and nobody has been allowed to damage what became the Ken Bates Dream, 'My Chelsea dream,' as he puts it.

2 Bates v. Harding

VICKY JARAMILLO OPENED THE FRONT DOOR of her Richmond flat and was delighted to see a courier holding a bottle of champagne. She signed for the celebration gift, thanked him, closed the door and went back inside to continue looking after her newborn baby.

She put the champagne alongside other bottles and gifts that she had accepted following the birth of Ella, the daughter she had just had with Matthew Harding, her married lover. She was happy, contented and without a care in the world.

What Vicky Jaramillo did not realise was that the man at the door was no ordinary courier. It was a plant, organised by Ken Bates. The man pretending to deliver the champagne had a camera hidden in his jacket and in those few moments of exchange Harding's lover was caught on film. 'The mistake she made was signing for the champagne,' explains Bates.

The pictures have never been used, and never will be. Bates, I understand, simply wanted confirmation of Harding's girlfriend, her name, signature and pictures. It was evidence. He wanted to put them with the growing file he had on the man known as 'the enemy'. Every bit of information helped him in his war with Harding, his fight to stay in complete control of Chelsea Football Club.

Bates explains: 'He had left his family home for two or three years. I know his people continually told him to go back to his wife Ruth and their children, to return to being a family man. When he left home he told Ruth never to go to Chelsea again.

I thought that was outrageous and immediately gave her two directors' box tickets. When Harding died, I made her a patron of the club.'

Again, I cannot emphasise enough the bitterness between these two men. The lengths they went to in order to undermine each other were extraordinary. Bates, for instance, often visited the Imperial Arms pub in the King's Road, Harding's favourite watering hole. Bates claims he introduced Harding to it. He would secretly send people over to film Harding inside the pub whenever he felt threatened and believed that he required new evidence. On one occasion he 'caught' Harding talking and joking with fans before leaving the pub and then returning half an hour later to have lunch with Spurs director Tony Berry.

Harding, I have discovered since his death, employed a public relations company to advise him on how to expose Bates in the media. He used the company for more than a year when the going got tough between them.

Chelsea discovered the ploy before he died and were aware that a lot of Harding's anti-Bates comments appearing in the media were generated by a paid employee. Bates has told me the name of the person who masterminded Harding's anti-Bates publicity machine but, for legal reasons, it would be impossible to reveal him. I would certainly have liked to have known this while the war was going on. It would have been good to have discovered which comments were sincere and from Harding himself and which comments were printed simply because a PR company said so.

Were we taken for a ride by Harding? Bates says yes: 'You guys helped him and I hope you are going to be big enough to admit it. You guys bloody well helped him.' Helped him? I would not say that, although there is no question that as a journalist you need information and, if Harding wanted to go on record about his rivalry with Bates, you would have been silly not to use the quotes. However, I take Bates's point and sympathise with him.

It had all begun so easily and calmly. Harding, the fanatical Chelsea fan who went from tea boy to multi-millionaire chairman of Benfield Insurance Group, met Bates for lunch after reading an advertisement in the *Financial Times*. It had been placed by Bates, outlining the club's plans on the pitch and the re-development strategy under Chelsea Village, the holding company. Bates, in turn, read an article in the same newspaper that listed Harding as the 60th richest man in the country. They met for the first time, over Guinness and oysters at The Imperial Arms, Harding's local – or so he said – in the King's Road. 'It was never Harding's pub. I introduced him to it. He lied that it was his local,' says Bates.

Bates told Harding that he needed help with financing the North Stand. Harding asked him how much and the reply was £7.5 million. Soon after their meeting Harding gave the club an interest-free loan of £5 million and the relationship was cemented. Harding explained to me that his money was given as convertible loan stock, which at some stage could become shares in Chelsea Village.

Bates was grateful to Harding for that loan and has never wavered in his thanks for the initial money that allowed the North Stand to be completed. Indeed, following his death, it was Bates's idea to name the stand after Harding and his name is emblazoned across it today.

Their relationship deteriorated following Harding's first meeting with Glenn Hoddle, now the England coach, whom Bates had plucked from Swindon and placed into the Premiership. Bates claims that in Hoddle, Harding saw the in-house relationship he needed to help him de-throne the king. Bates quickly became aware of the growing friendship between Harding and Hoddle and was wary of it. He grew to hate Harding, and distrust Hoddle. He was certainly not unhappy to see the back of Hoddle, when Glenn elected to accept the job as England coach, taking over from Terry Venables.

Bates says, 'I saw them becoming too friendly. In the end, Harding used Hoddle as a weapon against me. Harding worked hard on Hoddle. I didn't. I didn't have to. I was confident enough, there was no need for me to do anything other than be his chairman.

'The trouble with Matthew was that he was star struck. He liked to mix with the rich and famous. He never stopped talking about how rich he was. What does that indicate to you?'

Harding, because of his loan, had one foot inside the club. It was a giant stride, and Bates is convinced that from day one Harding's motivation was power – to become chairman and control the future of the football club. 'He wanted me out, plain and simple,' says Bates.

'He was working away behind my back all the time. He actually went to our bank and offered them a large sum of money to help him get rid of me. I believe that he did not want Chelsea to succeed – failure would have put pressure on me to resign. He even cultivated the Chelsea Independent Supporters' Association. He promised them everything, and they believed him.

'He actually said one match night that he hoped we would lose. "That would put real pressure on Batesy, wouldn't it?" he told someone, who in turn told me. It sounds like a true Chelsea fan, doesn't it?'

'By the end, I was not looking forward to going to Chelsea. He had made me feel unhappy at actually watching my own football club play. I was not having that. I do not react, then I overreact. I took so much stick and it hurt. But I jollied along for too long. I had a long-term plan and it certainly did not include him. What I had planned for Chelsea would never have included Harding.'

What Bates did not know was that Harding, too, had begun to grow weary of the fight with his arch rival. Slowly and carefully, friends and business associates had been persuading him to loosen his obsession with overturning Bates.

Indeed, Harding himself was, surprisingly, looking towards Southampton. His passion was still Chelsea but he realised, in the end, that he was never going to beat Bates.

One man who worked alongside him for the last ten months of his life was David Cooper, a City lawyer who became a friend and close associate. Cooper spent four full days with Harding every week, such was Harding's determination to find a way to force the change at Stamford Bridge. It dominated his thoughts. Every minute of every day he could not get Bates out of his mind.

Such was his hatred for the man that, yes, he would have preferred the club he loved to fail rather than be successful and give Bates more glory. It was a sickness that engulfed him. 'Matthew's passion was Chelsea but in the end he began to look towards Southampton,' Cooper reveals. 'His heart was with Chelsea but it was being broken.

'He was considering a five-year investment plan with the Saints, the club he called Little Chelsea on Sea.

'It amused me when Chelsea won the FA Cup and it was said that the team won it for Matthew. Don't make me laugh: he would have been horrified at their victory over Middlesbrough. Had it been a choice between winning the Cup with Bates and being relegated without him, he would have chosen the latter.

'He felt that a victory like the FA Cup would only add to the glorification of Bates and he could not have stood that. All that stuff about winning it for Matthew was crap.'

Cooper was introduced to Harding soon after Bates banned him from the directors' area of the club at the height of their war. Paul Miller, the former Spurs defender and friend of Harding who was then working for bankers Klienwort Benson, and John Gunn asked Cooper to sort out the mess. Harding desperately needed legal advice and assistance with his investments.

What Cooper found was a bubbly public figure who, on the inside, was eaten up by an obsession with Bates. Cooper adds: 'It was quickly apparent to me that the mess would never be sorted out on financial terms. Matthew was never going to gain control while Bates was there.

'My view was simple. What was the point in having a huge battle with Bates, because we knew that Bates would never stop fighting. I told Matthew that he did not have the time for a long, bloody fight, and I hoped that he did not have the inclination.

'It was far better for Matthew to protect his financial position and make that strong. He had no interest in the holding company, Chelsea Village. He was interested only in the football club and his position as vice chairman had to be safeguarded. Matthew would have preferred to have been chairman and part of the compromise was that Peter Middleton went on to the board of Chelsea.'

Bates, however, saw Middleton as a threat and quickly got rid of him. He thought, probably correctly, that Middleton was a plant by Harding. He did not like the man and it was not long before Middleton resigned. 'Yet on the day that Harding died, Middleton made his play and started a campaign to get control,' says Bates. 'That's the type of guy he is.' Cooper adds, 'I honestly believe that we had gone as far as possible. At one stage Bates did agree that Matthew could be chairman of the football club and then he changed his mind. Bates also said that he would review the situation in January 1997, but by then Matthew was dead and there was nothing to review. [Bates says that he had said to Matthew that he would reconsider the position in six months. 'But I was playing for time,' he says.]

'In life,' says Cooper, 'it is no good fighting brick walls, and that is what Matthew was doing. In the end, and after a lot of persuading, he accepted that he was always going to lose.

'Had he continued then he would have destroyed the value of his shareholding because if he went into a real battle, and Bates retaliated, as we know he would, the only sufferers would have been Chelsea Football Club. It would have been like taking money out of one pocket and putting it into another for Matthew.

'I told him that the best way to support the club was to keep his money behind them. At least then he would make capital out of it. Sooner or later Bates would have died, because that is a fact of life, and then the club would have been Matthew's.

'Matthew was certainly trying to push Bates too quickly. I kept telling him "Matthew, you are earning seven million pounds a year – why do you need this aggravation in your life? Why do you want to be associated with a man like this?"

'Had he come to me in the first place I would have told him that unless there was some very serious reason for doing it, don't. Do not get involved.

'I understand there were people who tried to stop him and he went ahead rather than listen. But it was his money and he was entitled to do what he liked with it. He believed that he could take day-to-day control of the football club. He forgot that Bates stood in the way. This really was the story of two huge egos. [Bates says, 'I have got an ego but he was egotistical. He was obsessed with me and everything I did.']

'When you analyse what went on it is an extraordinary situation. Here was Harding, a hugely successful man, someone with great charisma, a man who had scored politically with his one million pound gift to the Labour Party, and yet this thing with Bates dominated his life.

'I told him that life was too short. I told him that Bates was not his life, to relax his mood. It is not worth it. He was waking up with Bates and going to bed with him. It was mental torture. I stopped a lot of things and, in the end, I do believe the message was sinking through.'

It is incredible, isn't it, the extent of this hatred between two grown men? Bates is the godfather of Chelsea who runs the club from top to bottom. It is his club, he saved it and built it up, and no one is going to take it from him. And, in a way, he has a point. Harding, the new kid on the block, was young, ambitious – and jealous of Bates. And there the egos met. Crash, right in the middle.

It is interesting to analyse the characters. Bates, driven on by his desire to re-build Chelsea into the best, had only Chelsea to think about. It was, and still is, his life. He and his second wife Pam divorced and he now lives with girlfriend Suzannah Dwyer. Suzannah, he admits, has been good for him. 'She is good company and makes me laugh,' he says. There is no question that she has also taken some of the fire from him and that he has become a nicer, happier person, more contented with life. Or could that also have had a bit to do with Harding's death, his elimination from a war that was also beginning to affect Bates.

I have socialised with both men and, here again, their characters differed greatly. Bates, around a dinner table, likes to dominate the conversation, to be the centre of attraction, to drink good wine, perhaps some pink champagne to start with, and eat well. There is no doubting his generosity and on more than one occasion when we have been together he has picked up the tab, and paid it from a huge wad of notes pulled from a trouser pocket.

Harding, for all his money, was not a generous man: I cannot recall him once paying for the meals we shared and, on one occasion, he made me pay for a ticket in the North Stand when he had been banished there by Bates, after being banned from the boardroom. I was writing a colour piece about Harding, pushing his side of the story, and yet he insisted that I paid him before the match kicked off.

His lifestyle bore no comparison to that of Bates, who lived on his magnificent farm in Buckinghamshire and who is soon to move to a penthouse overlooking Stamford Bridge. Harding was happy with fish and chips at a greasy spoon, while Bates prefers a top restaurant. Harding loved to mix with the fans, downing pints of Guinness at his favourite pub, the Imperial Arms, before kickoff, while Bates mixed with opposing directors, sipping wine and exchanging football talk.

He was disgusted and horrified when Harding did return to the boardroom and often acted in a drunken way. 'It was yob behaviour,' Bates says. Harding often told me that he was not drunk, but just play-acting. 'They don't think I know what is going on,' he insisted. Was it all a game? Who knows? It was just part of the intricate story behind these two men, yet another round in Bates's fight to take Chelsea to the top – his way.

Harding left £202 million when he was tragically killed. Yet his lifestyle was not extravagant. Cooper explains: 'Bates has often said that Matthew had no money. That is bullshit. For a start, he didn't spend anything.

'He had a nice house in Sussex, but not substantial. He then bought a £400,000 house in Wimbledon for him and Vicky. Matthew had absolutely no interest in material things. I would show him an antique table worth thousands and he would say that it was just a table, nothing more.

'He could have bought anything but showed no interest. I once persuaded him to invest in a Brega watch. The top of the range is around £155,000 but instead he bought one for £9,000. Cars were the same. If they worked, that was enough. He drove a BMW and had an old Ferarri in the garage which he didn't drive.

'If he ate at the Savoy he would often ask for cheese on toast. If I went to football with him he would insist I paid for my ticket and a few days later he would ring up and remind me that I had still not paid. It was quirky. I would not call it meanness: it was just him.

'He ate out well at times, of course he did. He and Marco Pierre White, the restaurateur, were friends and I have seen Matthew pay a £500 bill for three and then tear up the receipt because it was an evening out with friends, and not a business-expenses lunch.

'He was certainly a complex character. On the other hand, he was extremely generous with charities, giving handsomely to anyone he thought needed a cash injection.'

You will find it amazing that Bates and Harding never really had a sensible conversation. They met across a boardroom table at times, and they exchanged comments at matches in the front row of the directors' box or in the boardroom while they entertained the opposing VIPs, but there were no in-depth, sit-down conversations. They never really tried to thrash this thing out man to man. 'It was impossible,' says Bates. 'In many ways Matthew was a very shallow man.'

Bates refutes the claim that Harding was a rich man. 'One of the five hundred richest men in England? I doubt it,' he says. 'I think that Matthew made the figures up as he went along.

'When he died he owed £25 million. He had shares in Chelsea and Benfields, that is all.

'The thing about Harding is that he had no cash, only assets, other people's assets. He was not a good businessman because he did not do his homework. He thought he could win but the waves came crashing back towards him. The more he tried the more they kept returning, and he couldn't understand that.

'He thought I would be swept away by his youthful enthusiasm, drive and money. He thought he could outmanoeuvre me; he thought the fans would turn against me – but he discovered that this old fool was not budging. Harding had loads of interests all over the world to see to. I only had one, Chelsea. It was mine and I was going to keep it.

'I will leave it to others to decide whether I am good at fighting. Someone once said that Ken Bates likes a good fight and if he has not got one he goes looking for one. That is not true. I am a good friend and a bad enemy. As I have said many times, I do not react, and then I overreact. My old headmaster once said about me, "Bates does not panic under pressure," and I have always remembered that.

'Harding came in without a plan, then he got ambitious. I know what was going on . . . and I have photographs . . . you have to be big enough to admit your mistakes and he never would. I knew about his love child long before the world did. I knew everything about him, without him realising.

'I told him straight away that I control one hundred per cent of the votes. He was constantly goaded by the press to challenge me. They told him that a media campaign helped drive the late Peter Swales out at Manchester City and they could help him get rid of Batesy.

'It didn't really get me down – it made me more determined. But when he started to stop me enjoying my football I knew enough was enough. I drove to the club that I love and something inside me was nagging away, not letting me enjoy what I had built. It was bloody Matthew Harding and I was not having that. No way.'

It was then that Bates began to hatch his plans to destroy Harding once and for all. He had decided to swat him out of the way. Bates adds, 'I knew if we went public, the shareholders thing would fall away. So he made two mistakes.

'He resigned from Chelsea Village, so he had no entitlement. His second mistake was that he would not convert his loan into shares.

'When we went on to the market it was a brilliant secret deal. On 1 March 1996, we had a meeting with Harding in which he wanted to outline his plans for us and the future. He was there with David Cooper, his solicitor, who is a bit arrogant and bumptious but nevertheless a clever man, and another advisor. He started to tell us what he intended to do.'

Yet again, Harding was to be beaten by Bates's secret file. A plan had been set up for Chelsea's solicitor, Mark Taylor, to produce a letter halfway through this meeting. Right on cue, with Harding in full flow, Taylor put his hand into his pocket and produced the document. 'It was a beautiful moment,' Bates says. 'Matthew was banging on about what he wanted and didn't want and, in the middle, Mark said that he had better read this, and gave him the letter.

'It was a twenty-eight-day notice that Chelsea were going public. Harding had been set up by me because he knew nothing about it. He went ape shit. He threatened to sue and went around the city trying to unrail our plans. He did everything he could think of.

'To fight, however, you have to have knowledge of what is happening. You also need to know how to fight. He didn't, I did. And I also had a lot of support. A lot of friends.'

One of those friends is Mark Taylor, a solicitor who has been welcomed into the Bates inner circle. Trust is a key word in the Bates dictionary and there is no question that Bates trusts Taylor. They first met in 1992 when Bates was at the end of his battle to save the ground against property developers Cabra Estates.

Bates had used the same lawyers for some time and felt that they had overcharged him. A good friend of Taylor's, Leon Gilewicz, was acting as his financial advisor, and Ken asked to be introduced to a lawyer. The club were about to purchase the lease of Stamford Bridge and Bates wanted someone he could trust. Taylor was recommended. 'Ken didn't really want a lawyer but knew he needed one,' recalls Taylor.

'The first time I acted for Chelsea was on that lease in 1992. I went to see Ken and he asked me how much I would charge to do two leases. I asked him how much the rent was and we agreed on a £30,000 fee. When we came to complete there were eighty-two competition documents. It was the worst deal I had done in my life. I am glad I did it, however, because the relationship has been good ever since.

'I discovered early on that he is one sharp boy. Ken is very astute with an amazingly quick brain. There is no question that he stuffed me on that deal.

'There are certainly two sides to Ken. There is the chairman who sits around the boardroom table and then there is the social animal. When you get underneath the tough exterior there is one of the nicest people you could wish to meet waiting to get out.

'We hated each other at the end of that first deal but now we are good friends and I have the utmost respect for him. To me he is nothing like the image often portrayed in the media. It was a great surprise when he invited me to become a director of the football club and it shows how much we have grown together since that initial fall out.'

It was Taylor whom Bates asked to join him at a very early meeting with Harding. 'Ken rang me and said that he had a meeting with someone who wanted to invest £5 million in the club, interest free. I thought that Ken was dreaming because no one does that. But, at the meeting in Chelsea Harbour, that is exactly what Harding did.

'I couldn't believe it. The silly thing about Matthew, and Peter Middleton, is that if they had stuck by what they said to Ken on day one of their involvement then Matthew would have been chairman of the football club within a few years, and Middleton chairman of Chelsea Village.

'The trouble is they couldn't wait and went behind Ken's back. That spelt danger.

'Matthew overlooked so much. Chelsea owns twenty-four per cent of the company and there is an investment trust in Guernsey which has been supportive of Ken from day one. They have enough shares to take over fifty-five per cent and Matthew failed to see this. He could not grasp that unless he could persuade the investment trust to back him rather than Ken, he would never take control. And it was not going to happen.

'What Matthew did when he couldn't get what he wanted was to run a smear campaign in the newspapers, and from day one he was being advised by a PR consultancy. That was outrageous – we couldn't believe that he would stoop so low.

'Matthew was naive. He underestimated the friendship, inside and outside Chelsea, towards Ken. He thought everyone in the club would be for him. What he forgot was that a lot of people were grateful to Ken Bates. Without him there would be no football club.

'It was all very well Matthew saying he was the saviour with his money, but where was he from 1982 to 1992 when it looked as though the club might go bust? No, Matthew did not come forward until everything had been resolved, when the way forward was apparent.

'Had Matthew held his fire, he would have got what he wanted. When he did come in, in 1993, Ken did not see him as a potential threat, certainly not as an enemy. The bottom line is that, from day one, Matthew Harding did not like Ken Bates.

'You have to give Matthew credit for giving Chelsea that initial £5 million loan. It enabled us to complete the building of the North Stand and kick-start the redevelopment. It was difficult to raise funds at that stage and Ken will always acknowledge that first loan.

'That five million was important and, after that, he lent the club other money, which was repaid to him. He did buy the ground, but it was no benefit to Chelsea because we still paid the same rent to Matthew.'

The stories from the two sides will never meet, will they? In one corner, Bates and his friends – and there are a lot of them. In the other corner there is now only David Cooper. Harding is not around to add his weight to the arguments that surround what is easily the most bitter feud there has ever been in football.

The Alan Sugar dispute with Terry Venables was fierce but it never grew to pure hatred, never got so personal that one side hired a PR company and the other compiled a file that included secretly taken photographs.

Cooper explains what Harding did for Chelsea and why: 'He bought the freehold of the ground and simultaneously rented it back. The cost of the interest on the freehold was repaid by the rent he got from the club. It put the freehold in safe hands.

'He granted a 990-year lease to Chelsea Pitch Owners which protected the pitch for ever. That saved it from being redeveloped and the ground is now owned by the supporters.

'He also made a loan to the club of £5 million, retaining a right to convert that into equity, which built the North Stand, now the Matthew Harding Stand. He converted the loan to shares. He also bought some more shares and took out some more share options. In the end, he was left with forty-one million shares, that is how many he owned when he died.

'They have carried in value from 73p to 170p and they are now at 98p [at the time of writing]. So he had 41 million at 98p. It turned out to be an extremely good investment. He didn't mind putting money into Chelsea and losing the interest because he knew he would get his money back in the end.

'He was not a philanthropist. He never intended to put money into Chelsea and down a black hole. It did take some persuasion by me, to get him to reinvest because, by then, he had fallen out with Bates. He did not want to invest any more in Chelsea because of the row.

'But the way the shares were structured in the club it was obvious that Matthew was never going to get control of the club.'

A huge bugbear with Harding and the people who worked for him was that they could not find out who owned the foreign shares in Chelsea Village. Cooper says, 'Whether Bates owns those foreign shares or not, he certainly has control over the voting shares. All we know is that Saffrey Champress, a firm of accountants in Jersey, hold the legal title. For whom they hold them we do not know. (Saffrey Champress were once the trustees of the offshore investment trust in Guernsey.)

'Bates would not tell us and I still have no idea. But there is a report in my office advising Matthew Harding not to invest any more money in the club because we could not get enough details of who actually owned the shares.'

Harding continually made an issue of this. And Cooper now says he would love the answer to one question. How did Bates manage to get Chelsea public on the AIM with that lack of information? Bates says that the so-called mystery men are the same people who were there when Harding's people ran their own check on the company before Harding's initial investment.

While Bates argues that Harding hardly put anything into Chelsea, Cooper says it was up around £30 million. He explains: 'The freehold cost was £16 million, then there was the £5 million in the North Stand and then his shares.

'The freehold has been sold back, at a discount, but we wanted out of that. No one is apologising that Matthew doubled his money in his investment.'

The Harding estate, which is run by the appointed executors Mark Killic and Maggie Nugent, still owns £40 million worth of shares, a 24 per cent holding in Chelsea Village. Cooper says, 'There is no representation on the board because he [Bates] will not have it. No one can force him.

'Those forty million shares are on the market and we are looking for a single purchaser. If Bates wants to put them in friendly hands we have told him that they are on the market. Since Matthew died, 100,000 have been sold to small investors.

'The person who buys the forty million would get almost twenty-five per cent of the company. Eventually, he or she might have the opportunity to take control of the company. It might give them enough to make a bid in due course for the shares which are outstanding. Who knows? I suspect that Bates will sell sooner or later.

'I do not believe that Harding's forty million shares will get into the wrong hands. To be fair to Bates, if he has done nothing else he has steered the club, since 1982, into a solid situation.

'Matthew, when he died, left everything for Mark and Maggie to distribute as they felt fit, with a letter of wishes to look after Ruth and the kids and Vicky and the kids, plus the shareholders of Benfield. I am in touch with them all and talk regularly to Ruth.

'I just cannot understand this thing about him not having money. I have it in black and white, the records of Benfield and the accounts showing his income. It's clear as a bell. He earned his money very quickly and was taking home seven million a year when he died. There was a £3.5 million salary and a £3.5 million dividend. Matthew owned a third of Benfield.'

Taylor says of the Harding shares, 'Yes, we know they are on the market. Harding's executors have put out an instruction to their stockbrokers to sell once the price reaches 115p a share. We keep an eye on the situation but cannot stop anyone selling. It is a free market and you are talking about a public company.

'If someone came along and wanted to buy them all I am sure we would be consulted. If someone did not consult us first then he would be fairly stupid. One or two have been sold but the majority remain. Clearly, we would rather they were not sold as one block.'

Another thing that Bates and Harding fell out over was the redevelopment of Stamford Bridge. Harding wanted a 60,000-capacity stadium with not so much emphasis on the hotel, penthouses and Chelsea Village scheme. He felt that the more success the club achieved, the more people would want to watch. He believed that putting in the hotel and flats, which would squeeze the capacity to around 44,000, would lead to public frustration and a missed opportunity of revenue. 'There was one hell of a row over that,' admitted Cooper.

Harding, it seemed, had a point. Manchester United and Newcastle, boasting two of the finest stadiums in the Premiership, cannot meet the demand for tickets. Arsenal are desperate to move from their Highbury home because they could sell out twice over for every home game. But if Harding had done his homework he would have realised that the council would not allow it. A new stand would have been too high, blocking out the light for local residents.

Bates had his dream to fulfil. When he took over he had it in his mind's eye and then in 1992, when the ground was secured, he produced a model of exactly what Chelsea would look like going into the millennium. It sat in his office at Stamford Bridge and almost every other visitor was shown the model, with its adjoining hotel, restaurants, flats, penthouses, and megastore. Most people, at that stage, looked at it admiringly but thought, 'Good try, Ken, but you will never do it.'

That was certainly my attitude and even Mark Taylor admits, 'When I saw it in 1992 I thought that Ken was in dreamland. Five years later it was all there. Now we are nearing completion, with the second hotel opening in May 1999 and the whole lot finished by the end of that year. It has been a fantastic achievement by him, a dream come true.'

Bates's Chelsea dream began when he bought the club for £1 in 1982 and he vowed then to fight to the end to achieve it. Some, like Harding, have tried to wrestle it away from him but all have failed.

Now that it is over, Bates often reflects on the war that he says he did not want and did not start. He once asked me, 'Why did Matthew do it? What was the point?'

For the first time, he reveals exactly when he realised that Harding was after him big time: 'I was in Zaragoza for our European Cup Winners' Cup semi-final first leg under Hoddle.' There had been a couple of incidents that had unsettled him. Just before the trip he had been approached by a journalist and asked if he was selling out for £15 million. 'Don't be stupid,' was the reply, but something nagged at him.

Then, on the airport tarmac in Zaragoza, I approached Bates on behalf of the other journalists on the trip and asked him about Harding and a sell out. We had also heard the rumours. The reply was the same but, yet again, it worried Bates. He rang me that afternoon, asking me where the information had come from and why I had asked the question.

The following day, Bates and Harding had lunch. Bates recalls: 'At that lunch I told Matthew that in the year 2002 I would have been in charge for twenty years and that it might be the perfect time for him to take control. I told him that I would go on a three-month cruise so that he could get his feet under the table with no interference and media attention. Well, Matthew went berserk. Clearly, he had no intention of waiting that long.'

The war had begun, even if it did not hit the media until later. Harding started to do little things that got under Bates's skin, like use his private table at the Savoy. It sounds silly now, but it was all part of the war.

But Bates has never got the answers he craved. Why did Matthew Harding go to war in such a way? Why did he hate Bates so much? He died before Bates could get to the bottom of it. There is no question that it nags him to this day and although he won he often feels it was a victory without meaning. It was a fight that grew and grew without his really knowing why. The two men hardly talked to each other – they just fought in public. 'But I was always reacting to Harding,' says Bates. 'I never instigated any of it.'

3 You Will Never Beat Ken Bates

ATTHEW HARDING PINNED DAVID MELLOR against a wall inside the House of Commons, clutched him by the arm and said threateningly, 'Are you with me or against me? Are you with him or me?'

Harding was drunk, aggressive and intimidating. Mellor had not seen him quite like this before and was shocked. Harding continued, 'If you are not with me then you will never be welcome at Chelsea when I take over.'

The incident, following a dinner for Paul Elliott, the former Chelsea player whose career was cut short by injury, will never be forgotten by Mellor. The former Conservative MP and Heritage Secretary was appalled. He says, 'I had to ask Matthew that after all I had been through in my life did he really think I was going to succumb to that sort of behaviour?'

Harding, however, had not finished his attack, as Mellor recalls. 'He literally lashed out at me. He said that I was a self-appointed fan of the club and that I had criticised Chelsea in the past. I will always remember the incident.

'It made me feel uneasy. I felt uneasy being part of a set-up where a guy can behave like that. I would never have had the money of Matthew Harding, indeed never will have, but I was not some little slug for him to kick around the garden. He, clearly, must have thought I was.'

I find this story more interesting than any other about Harding. We have heard before about his drunken behaviour, in the boardroom at Chelsea, embarrassing Bates and the

Chelsea directors, and in his favourite watering holes around London. It was not uncommon to witness Harding, in the Imperial Arms before kickoff, singing, dancing, shouting, swearing and spilling his Guinness with other supporters. Bates reveals that once, at Sheffield Wednesday, the directors had to take him to hospital because he was so drunk. He was a man of the people and no one can ignore the game's response, country-wide, when he died. They would not have believed the lengths he had gone to, behind the scenes, to get at Bates.

But Mellor discovered a darker side to him. Here was a desperate man, cornered by Bates's determination, a man looking for a way to bring an opponent down. Here was a man near to violence, certainly violence of the tongue. It was a side I certainly had not seen or been told about before.

It was a Matthew Harding realising he was never going to win control of Chelsea. He had been told that no one beats Ken Bates and this truth was beginning to dawn on him. But pinning a respected public figure up against a wall and threatening him is strange behaviour indeed. Bates says, 'When Matthew was drunk, he was a yob. When he was sober, he was devious.'

A week later the two men met again and this time Harding's mood had changed and he apologised for his behaviour. Mellor adds, 'We embraced and he said that he had been a cunt. He said he was sorry. I was still uneasy, though, and I felt like that long after.

'The trouble with Matthew was that he was a control freak. Ken is assertive but does not react against everything you say. He does not feel that unless you agree with him you have no part in his life.

'He has always given me the respect I am entitled to after what I have achieved in my life. I can tell Ken Bates he is wrong, and have done so many times. He does not have to agree but that is life. Matthew came through a world where no one had said boo to him and he could not cope with someone like Ken standing up to him. He had to get what he wanted.'

The more Harding tried, the more people told him that he would never unseat Bates. The harder he pushed, the more determined Bates became that he would never gain control.

Others also underestimated the staying power of Bates. When Harding did a deal with the Royal Bank of Scotland, Bates went to them and asked, 'Why did you do it?' He recalls: 'They were honest in their reply. They didn't beat about the bush and said that I was sixty-three and he was forty-one. They thought they had a better chance of getting their money back off him. Nothing personal, they said.'

Nothing personal? But, oh, it was. Very personal. Bates not only proved the bank wrong, he proved anyone who doubted his stubbornness, character and determination wrong, too. The bottom line is that he invited Harding in and then fell out with him, big time. He fell out with him because of one thing – power. Harding wanted to de-throne the king and couldn't. Bates now sneers: 'Harding said he was a lifelong supporter. Bollocks.

'Where was he when I was fighting tooth and nail to save the club. Since 1982 I have spent seven days a week, sometimes seventeen hours a day, working for Chelsea. How many years is that? That is a fan, a supporter, someone who cares. Not some johnny-come-lately.'

Mellor was a Chelsea fan who defected to Fulham because of the racism and crowd trouble at Stamford Bridge in the seventies. He was then invited, and wooed, back by Bates when he took over. Here was another person caught right in the middle of the bloody war. His insight is interesting: 'People often said to me "Why didn't Matthew and Ken get on?" Without glamorising it too much, it is rather like a march through London or any other city. People who were with Ken on the march were very much for him. Those who were not, he queried their motives.

'I will never understand why Matthew, if he felt that strongly about the club, did not come off the terraces or out of his seat as a supporter earlier. He could so easily have thrown his weight behind the club earlier. And he would have been a big help when things were tough for the club, and Ken in particular.

'Ken regarded him as a useful guy to have around, until they fell out. Matthew had no right to claim that he was Mr Chelsea when that certainly was Ken Bates. Had it not been for Bates, the bulldozers would have arrived and ploughed right through the club and ground, with Matthew still sitting in his supporter's seat in the East Stand.

'Some of us tried to sort the problems out, but they became too deep. Matthew unkindly tried to portray Ken as someone who simply lived off the club, rather than someone who was the driving force behind it. Matthew used that view to rationalise his own position.

'Matthew always said to me that he was the saviour, and would not see it any other way. He said to me that none of the institutions would lend money to Ken Bates, and he really believed that.

'He said many times, "If I'm not here, there will be no money invested. I am the one who can save Chelsea Football Club."'

I can confirm this inner belief that Harding had. A week before he died, he and I shared an evening at a pub close to his home in Wimbledon. He insisted that night that, 'It will be a matter of public record one day that Glenn Hoddle and I saved Chelsea Football Club.' He simply had no respect for Bates and would not recognise anything that he had done, or was doing.

Mellor adds, 'In my many conversations with Matthew I would say to him that Ken was in his sixties and he was barely forty. Why did he not try and negotiate a period well into the distance when there could be a takeover, or at least an agreement?

'Ken had said at one stage that he might be willing to step down at seventy. I am never sure, when that moment comes, whether he will be ready to go, or want to go, or, indeed, if he should go.

'I encouraged Matthew to be Bates's loyal deputy and have some future agreement to take over. It is not unlike Peter Mead waiting his turn to take control at Millwall. Peter may not have always been happy with the way Reg Burr handled things, but there was never a war, and he waited his turn.

'I am sure Matthew's intentions were good but he wanted it to be him and him alone. "It is me." It was his motto.

'Ken did not trust Matthew, or Glenn Hoddle for that matter. Ken felt that Matthew was suborning people at the club and I have to say here that I have no reason to suggest that Glenn knew it was happening. But Matthew told me many times, "Glenn will not stay if Ken does." Glenn and Matthew had an understanding and this, of course, got back to Ken. I have no doubt that Matthew also tried to suborn Colin Hutchinson.

'I took the sensible view that intelligent people could work it out in the end. I believed that one day Matthew would realise this. But now I have my doubts whether they would ever have got on.

'Matthew thought that he could force out Ken through fan power. He thought the fans would turn on Bates and was surprised, and bitterly disappointed, when they didn't. He believed that the fans would realise that Ken wouldn't have the resources to buy the star players for Chelsea to become a really big club.

'He liked it when people referred to him as the man with the money bags. But, as we know, money does not solve all problems. You need judgment too.

'Matthew, as a shrewd businessman, simply did not grasp two things – that Bates controlled all votes and, also, he underestimated Bates's ruthless streak. Bates would just say to Matthew, "OK then, fuck off." And he meant it. He barred him from the club to prove it.

'Matthew assumed that Ken would not see it through. And how many men would have the balls to do it, and risk all the back-page headlines that went with it? There was a lot of nastiness.

'When Matthew was being outmanoeuvred and Ken was away on a business trip he said, "Ken has got nothing to do but run Chelsea. I have all my other things."

'But Harding was missing the point; Bates was determined and he had all the time in the world to be just that. He could organise not only Chelsea's future, but also the plan to keep out Harding. Matthew, it now seems, was a complex character behind the shiny surface that we saw so often.'

Mellor recalls a lunch they shared: 'When we sat down, he ordered a bottle of white immediately and told the waiter that in forty-five minutes exactly he wanted a bottle of red. He was laying out an agenda that I would bow to. I felt sorry for him in the end.'

Like many powerful men on this earth, he could not cope with silly, trivial things going wrong, like a clock that had stopped or a light bulb that needed replacing. Silly things that can make a man lose his concentration and then his grasp on the big-business world in which he lives. Harding could not stand it if the waiters at the Savoy did not give him ten minutes exactly between each course. And it had to be ten minutes, not nine or eleven, but ten. If they got it wrong, he gave them terrible public stick. He also loved tomato ketchup and ate it with everything. If a restaurant didn't have any, he never went back.

Mellor does not believe that there could ever have been an agreement between Harding and Bates. 'My mother used to say that you cannot have two cocks in one barnyard. I am sorry to say that Matthew and Ken were born to hate each other.

'Had Matthew lived, he might never have achieved what he wanted, unless there had been a massive personality change. What he did have and it could have been a huge asset for him – and it is something that Ken never has had – is the ability to be loved by all supporters of football. He was one of them, even to those fans who had never met him, and that cannot be taken lightly.'

Matthew Harding died in a helicopter crash on 22 October 1996. He was returning from a Chelsea game in Bolton when the aircraft came down in the early hours of the morning in foggy conditions. I was up all that night with my own office calling every half-hour and, by the time it was light, everyone was asking for confirmation that it was Harding. It was.

The days that followed were very emotional for the club. That very afternoon, Chelsea held a press conference and Bates, to his credit, handled the situation magnificently. He has a history of saying the wrong things in public but this time there was not a sentence out of place and he announced that the North Stand would become the Matthew Harding Stand. He led the press conference and gave radio and television interviews with dignity and composure when, deep down, his feelings would have been very different.

Bates has never shed a tear for Harding, and why should he? He felt that here was a real enemy. Harding was trying to oust him, by fair means and foul, and there is no question that Bates is pleased that Harding is out of the way. Yes, it was a tragedy, but clearly something had to happen to separate the two.

Had Harding lived, the war would have been going on today. Harding would have fought for control and Bates would have resisted strongly. There would have been many more arguments and massive amounts of publicity between the pair. The biggest sufferer would have been Chelsea Football Club. There is no question that the war, while it lasted, damaged the club and it would have continued to do so.

Mellor adds, 'I hate to think what would have happened had Matthew lived. I woke that morning of the helicopter crash and knew straight away that it was Matthew. Something told me as soon as I heard the news of a helicopter crash.

'I rang my ex-wife, Judith, and told her that something terrible had happened. Judith has been very close to Matthew's wife, Ruth, and I told her to ring Ruth. I shed a tear, of course I did. Even though Matthew and I were never bosom pals, never as close as I am with Ken, I was terribly sorry he died.'

Bates was not sorry. He believes that it was meant to be. He had been worried for a long time over how he was going to end the war. He had banned Harding, criticised him, taken him on behind the scenes and proved that he did not have a hope of power control at Stamford Bridge, but his opponent would not go away. In the end, the decision was made for him.

As David Webb, one of Bates's eight managers in sixteen years of power, once said, 'You never beat Ken Bates. It doesn't matter who you are. He is Mr Chelsea and anyone with ambitions of taking him on has to realise that. He is not for breaking. In the end, he didn't want me, but I have a lot of time for him. I respect the bloke for what he has done for that club.'

Bates is now stronger than ever. There will be no more fights because everything is secured – the ground, the finance, the future. Bates says, 'Having just seen off Harding, I'm not going anywhere. I still enjoy it and Chelsea will grow and grow under me. I had enough of Harding, enough, enough.

'When I walk into my penthouse home overlooking Chelsea I will say to myself, all the fights were worthwhile. All the fights with Cabra, Marlar, Harding, everyone. They are all out of the way. Thank God.

'I can look back with pride and justification on what I have done. Chelsea Football Club is all that mattered and the club is the real winner, not Ken Bates. I still enjoy what I do and I intend to enjoy it for a few more years yet. I have huge ambitions for this club and nothing is going to stop us now.

'There is no one left to stand in the way. There is no one who wants to pick a war with Ken Bates. The others failed. They should have known better.'

4 'Do You Want To Buy Chelsea Football Club?'

I T WAS MALCOLM ALLISON, the former Manchester City and Crystal Palace manager, who indirectly began the Ken Bates era at Chelsea. Allison and Bates were with a group of friends, exchanging drinks, gossip and laughter, when a lady in the company caught the eye of Bates. 'Who is that man?' she asked a friend. 'Can I be introduced to him?'

Allison did the introductions and, without knowing, the Chelsea dream had started. The lady was June Mears, wife of Brian, the former Chelsea chairman. She and Bates got on and it was not long before June invited Ken and his then wife, Pam, to Stamford Bridge.

Bates explains: 'I was living in Monte Carlo at the time but maintained an interest in Oldham Football Club. Malcolm Allison and I knew each other and kept in touch. He is a very sociable bloke, even if he is a bit expensive. He said that if ever I wanted to watch Palace to give him a call. I did one day, and that is when the drinks party began, the one with June Mears there. She was a sociable person, and quite a laugh.'

The friendship grew between the Bates and the Mears and Ken and Pam were invited to the Mears's son's 21st birthday party. It was on that evening that Bates offered to sponsor every London derby played at Stamford Bridge. The club had just been relegated under the late Danny Blanchflower and Bates, on the spur of the moment, offered to help. He flamboyantly wrote out a cheque for £18,000.

It was a gesture that friends, opponents and anyone else

connected with football have grown to accept as part of the Bates style.

Bates says, 'I was always a football person and first got involved at Oldham. Freddie Pye, a former business partner of mine, asked me to help him out. I bought it from him and put a few bob into the club to help them get going. It was difficult for me to get involved completely because Oldham was a long way to travel for every home game. I did let it be known that if a club ever came up in the London area, and I liked it, I would be interested.'

Bates's friendship with the Mears developed but it was another business associate, a man called Martin Spencer, who alerted Bates to Chelsea. Spencer asked Bates if he would be interested in buying Chelsea. Bates recalls: 'I asked him what the problem was and Martin explained that the club was going into receivership and that he was acting for them. I was shocked because the name of Chelsea had always been linked with exciting players and success.

'Martin and I had a meeting and he said that he was worried because no one at the club would really take the situation seriously enough. He told me that Chelsea, at the start of that season, needed £300,000 to survive.'

Chelsea had a good run in the FA Cup, which allowed them to bank some extra money, but the inevitable crunch was coming and Spencer brought the two parties together, Bates and the Chelsea directors.

By that time, Bates had fallen out with the Mears. 'At one stage I couldn't even get a lunch table in the restaurant for a London derby that I had sponsored, which I thought was a bit of a cheek,' he explains.

Brian Mears was the Chelsea chairman and his half-brother, David, was also on the board and at the meeting with Bates to discuss a possible takeover. 'I found David a funny fellow and didn't quite know how to take him,' says Bates. 'It wasn't long before he said that he didn't think that Chelsea could do business with me. Fair enough, I thought, and went my way.'

Spencer, however, realised how serious the problem was. One of football's most famous clubs was falling apart. The main stand, built under the Mears's guidance, had run massively over budget and had become a noose around their necks. Spencer persuaded David Mears and Bates to have another meeting, this time at the office of the club's lawyers.

Bates recalls: 'David said to me that he didn't think that there was time to resolve anything at the meeting that day. He asked if I would put down £300,000 adding that the other details would be sorted out later.

'I looked at him as if he was mad. I said, "If you think I'm going to put an unsecured loan into a club that's going bankrupt, and leave prats like you in charge, then you've got another think coming." Typical Bates. Straight to the point. 'What is the benefit of going around the houses?' he says. 'Say what you think.' And he always does.

In Chelsea's next match they were knocked out of the FA Cup, 3–2 at home, by Spurs. On the Monday morning, the club's bank manager rang Spencer and told him that he had two cheques in his hand, one for the Football Association's share of the gate receipts on Saturday, and the other one to pay the players' wages. 'Which one do you want me to bounce?' he asked Spencer. The receiver told him to pay the FA because the players could always be paid a week late.

On the Friday, four days later, Bates and Chelsea met again. 'Spencer told me that the deal would be done at 8.30 that night,' says Bates. 'These kinds of deals are always finished before the weekend, when lawyers realise they are late for an appointment with their wives, or the accountant has to go down to Hampshire for a weekend retreat.' Spencer, in the end, was fifteen minutes out, and it was 8.45 when Ken Bates became the owner of Chelsea Football Club. 'We did in forty-five minutes what we had been buggering about with all day,' he says. It was 2 April 1982. 'It was the Friday before the team played Oldham, my old club, in one of those strange coincidences.'

Bates bought Chelsea for £1 but inherited debts of more than £2 million.

It had taken eleven weeks of negotiating for Bates to get his hands on Chelsea. The holding company, SB Properties, continued to own the ground. Bates initially leased the stadium from the holding company for a seven-year period. Bates said in one of his opening speeches, 'I have ensured that football will be played here for as long as the team justify it and the fans want it. We can now think in terms of next season rather than next week. If, at the end of the lease, the ground is available, we can buy it from the holding company.'

The wheeling and dealing had begun. The negotiations were under way and Ken Bates's Chelsea dream had started. 'I knew what I wanted from that day,' he says. 'I could see the rise and rise of the club in my mind. I recall standing in the middle of the pitch after completing the takeover and thinking to myself, one day . . . one day.'

Even then, Bates was described as one of the most colourful and controversial entrepreneurs in football. He was a successful businessman at the age of 21, opening a successful tipping and haulage concern in London. It later expanded into quarry interests.

Later, he ran a large ready-mix concrete company in the north, basing himself in Blackburn, where he built up a series of businesses covering finance, boat building and electronics. He moved to the Virgin Islands, where he managed a public company before settling in Dublin. An article in the *Financial Times* in 1964 described him as making a fortune in ready-mixed concrete. Bates was quoted in the article as saying, 'I did it by breaking all the rules.'

Bates took over as Oldham chairman at Christmas 1965 but in 1968 he resigned. The then vice chairman, Harry Massey, said, 'He was too ambitious too quickly. His pace was just too fast.' To this day, that pace has never dropped. It is remarkable how he has retained his fight and his enthusiasm. Certainly, right from the start at Chelsea he was in a hurry to put the club back on its feet.

Bates says curtly, 'I discovered all the way through that there were a lot of people who did not want me to succeed. I am convinced I was sold the club by the old regime with them believing that I would fail. Indeed, they wanted me to. Nice, isn't it? To be sold a club with the sellers hoping that the buyer makes a hash of it.

'Brian and June Mears were the first to have that feeling and the list went on. I was friendly with them once, before I went the same way as most of June's friends. I was slung out of her inner circle.

'It was interesting. I had no idea how to buy a football club when this started, but here I was, owning Chelsea. I had a feeling of, OK, let's get on with it.

'I bought the football club and took over the debts. When I moved in, Chelsea were losing £12,000 a week. They were a disgrace. As a business, they were committing suicide.

'I recall sitting in what was then my office and asking myself, Can I do it? Yes, I bloody well can. And I did, and I have.'

The job Bates has done is emphasised by these extraordinary figures. The club that was going nowhere, with £2 million debts and losing £12,000 a week, has been transformed into a successful organisation with an annual turnover of £80 million. It is an amazing achievement, an amazing story.

At his first match as the new owner, Bates got an invitation from Lord Chelsea to have lunch before the kickoff. 'Come as my guest,' said Lord Chelsea. 'That's nice of you,' said Bates. 'Actually, it is my club.' This, says Bates, illustrates just how the club was run.

'When I arrived for lunch there were seventeen of us sitting around the table. Seventeen! There were grandchildren, friends . . . hangers-on. Out came the cigars and top of the range brandy. The bill was £500, and this was the lot who couldn't pay the players' wages. It was scandalous and I told them so.

'There were hangers-on in the wrong areas, all over the club. I wrote everything off and started again. Chelsea used to have a bootman to clean the boots. The apprentices just stood around watching him clean away. He went. The directors had their own chauffeur to drive them around town. He went. Even the lottery lost money. How? There were just two birds selling tickets. They went.

'It was probably around that time that I decided to dig in, come what may. I was buggered if they were going to kill off Chelsea behind my back.

'I looked only at the upside and thought that here was an

opportunity too good to miss. If Chelsea could be turned around, we were looking at one of the great clubs in the country. I did not realise at that stage that it would take so long to achieve.

'But there I was, sitting on twelve acres of prime London site, a few miles from Harrods, on the King's Road, and with no real competition from other clubs, and yet the club was in a mess. Sod it, I am going to fight to make Chelsea great, I told myself. They should be on their own, right up there, I thought.

'Chelsea had under-achieved for too long. No one had been interested in the football. They had used it as a social club, somewhere to pleasure themselves at the cost of others. It was a disgrace. Now they were trying to sell it off.

'The Mears family did not want me to succeed. The more success I had, the more it reflected badly on themselves.'

Horrendous fights followed. Bates explains: 'Mears sold out to Noonan at Marlar Estates. Robert Noonan was an opportunist who ran his operations from Ireland. He put planning permission in to turn Stamford Bridge into a residential area. I was not having that. Initially, the Tory council supported the bid.

'Duggan didn't want football at Stamford Bridge. He had no feeling for the sport whatsoever. What he wanted to do was sell Stamford Bridge, buy out QPR and merge them with Fulham at Craven Cottage. He wanted to call them Fulham Park Rangers. Then he could ship us across West London to Loftus Road. Eventually, he would have sold that ground off too and made himself £300 million.

'Before Harding, this man Duggan was my toughest opponent. He had absolutely no love or feeling for Chelsea or their supporters. I was fighting back hard by this time and there were no rules. It was bloody dirty. I knew that if I didn't win there would be no Chelsea. Just houses.'

Just like Harding, Duggan and the others did not realise the power of Bates, or the determination. The first thing Bates did was block the merger between QPR and Fulham. He was then a member of the Football League Committee and pointed out to the other members that a merger would mean the introduction of a newly formed club, and that was not allowed. 'That killed that little plan off, and I had to get rid of a lot more down the years,' says Bates.

What Bates discovered was that, behind his back, people were scheming. He was the owner, but the power stayed with others, like the Mears family. Bates built up his own network of spies and people he could trust. Trust has been a key word in his fight. He has only ever wanted like-minded people on his side, and he has no thoughts or warmth for anyone who does not share his commitment. He once told me, 'I am now like a spider sitting in the middle of my web. All the legs lead out to people I know and trust and those people bring me back the information. I know everything going on where my club is concerned.

'I have come up against a lot of devious and dishonourable people. No doubt others will look at my methods and level criticism, but at least I had one thing on my mind throughout – the future of the club. And when I had made sure Chelsea were safe at Stamford Bridge, I began building them into the best. No one can criticise me for that.

Bates discovered that, among the shareholders, David Mears had forty per cent of the shares, Brian nine per cent, Thompson four or five and then there were other, smaller shareholders scattered around. 'Mears sold out to Marlar. June was courted by Noonan and sold out to him,' explains Bates.

'Meanwhile, I had been going around gobbling up all the small shares. In the end, I had twenty-eight per cent and they had seventy-two. There was also the company that owned the ground on which we had a seven-year lease with an option to buy. Also, the council had backed the bid to turn the stadium into houses.' The fight was on.

Bates needed friends, people he could trust. People who could help him. Enter David Mellor. It was Mellor, using the power of his position as MP for Putney, who persuaded the council to change their mind about the future of Chelsea. His story about Bates and the wars inside and outside Stamford Bridge is interesting.

Mellor explains: 'I was brought up in Dorset and although I was a football fan my loyalties to clubs fluctuated as a boy. We had no real local team. It was a godsend when, at twenty-one I graduated from Cambridge and moved to London and found myself living a stone's throw from Chelsea. It was the obvious place for me to go and watch football and I stood in the Shed with my mates and watched Ossie, Hudson and all the others in that great side.

'At that stage one assumed that the club would just go from strength to strength. I followed them intently. Even when I married in 1974 and moved out of the city, I still followed and watched them closely.

'There is no question that at the end of the Mears era they were in bad shape. They lacked direction, on and off the pitch. There was also the growing problem of hooliganism in the country, linked directly with football. I am not a namby-pamby and my language is not always the best but I do not like racism and I do not like violence.

'The problem culminated for me at a Chelsea game against Spurs. A Spurs fan sitting in front of me was being particularly obnoxious. When Spurs scored, another fan, this time sitting behind me, leant over me and hit the guy in front full in the mouth. I thought to myself then, 'Do I really need this?'

It was the end of the Mellor love affair with football, at least for the time being. When, in 1980, he was elected MP for Putney and again moved closer to London, he decided that Fulham would be the club for him.

'I followed Fulham for two seasons. They were a good side and had three outstanding young players, Geoff Hopkins, Paul Parker and Ray Houghton. They almost got promotion under Malcolm Macdonald but it became obvious that the club was not something Clay was prepared to invest in. I became disillusioned even though the crowd, at that time, were nicer to be involved with than at Chelsea.

'Chelsea came to Craven Cottage in that season and beat Fulham 5–3. It was a smashing game of football. It brought home to me the phrase, form is temporary, class is for ever.' It was the match that was to change Mellor's sporting life. It was here that he was introduced to Bates, forming a relationship that has grown from that day.

Mellor continues: 'In the boardroom after the game I was introduced to Bates. He came over and said, "You are Chelsea really, aren't you?" I said yes and he added, "Come back, I need you, Chelsea are a shambles, a mess." He was aware of who I was – it was the MP for Putney he was talking to at that stage, not just David Mellor.

'I explained the reason I had left and he quickly intervened, saying, "I have no time for that. It was the old regime. I am different to Mears and we can co-operate with the police. Come on, come back." So I went back to Chelsea. Really, I went home.

'I went back as a supporter more than an MP but I made it clear to Ken that I would help him with any problems he had.

'I soon discovered the difference between Ken and Ernie Clay. Ken was made offers by the property company men, huge offers, but he didn't accept them. Ken, basically, proved to be a man of his word. That is why I have time for him. He could so easily have sold out.

'Throughout the eighties, football was in the doldrums and Stamford Bridge was a valuable piece of property. It was a great asset, worth more as a site than a football club. It could so easily have been used to make a lot of money but Bates resisted. He once said to me, "Why don't these people realise, there are only three things I care about – my family, my farm and my football club." Without Ken Bates there would be no Chelsea Football Club.'

By the late eighties, Bates had spent more than £2 million on legal fees, just fighting to keep hold of the football club. Mellor has only respect for him: 'He is a real bastard to get in a tangle with. He knew the score of business and was completely ruthless. He used the Companies Act at every opportunity. There are unattractive sides to him, of course there are. But the people who took him on didn't realise how sharp he was.

'I have looked back and thought about that chance boardroom meeting many times. He told me something on that occasion that, fifteen years on, has been vindicated. He said he was going to win and turn Chelsea into the best. I have been glad to be part of that.

'It is probably why he and I are friends. I was with him all those years ago when the chips were down. Anyone can be with him now. But he likes loyalty. It was bloody difficult in those early days.

'I hope that he mentions me in the same context. I went back to Chelsea as an active supporter, willing to advise and help where I could.

'There was a lot of hostility towards the club, especially from local residents. A lot of people, however, bought their house at a lower price because the ground is there, but then complained that it was there.

'The only way the club could be saved was for the Bridge to be bought from the clutches of the property developers. Then would come a good planning permission to generate resources.

'There was a public inquiry and that is when Ken was glad to have me on board. I spoke up for the club, arguing the case that Chelsea had to be saved. I got a lot of stick and one Hammersmith Councillor, Martin Howe, wrote me a vicious letter, criticising me for sticking up for the club and going against local opinion. He told me to keep my nose out of it but, as a football fan, I was entitled to speak up for the club that I love. I was also a Member of Parliament for a neighbouring constituency. I felt I could say what I wanted for three reasons. One, why should I not speak up for the club? Two, my constituency was made up of a huge number of Chelsea fans, so I was sticking up for them and, three, I was going in to bat for better amenities in London. Had I been MP for Highbury, I would have fought for Arsenal, had they been in trouble.'

The protesters' answer was that Chelsea should be given a ground – somewhere on the M25. 'I ask you,' adds Mellor, 'did these people have no feelings for the supporters?

'I had lunch with Duggan – and I have to say that we have since become friends – and I shocked him with my forthright approach. I think even Ken was surprised with how strongly I felt about it. It was at about the same time that the Mary Rose Theatre was discovered under a site in the city and a number of luvvies were protesting. I told Duggan that it would make the Mary Rose protests look like a teddy bears' picnic if he ever tried to put the bulldozers into Chelsea.'

Duggan, however, was set. He had agreed to buy the land and he already had a major builder lined up to put houses on the site. Duggan, in fact, warned Mellor off. He said that it was always the same, people complaining about development. Mellor recalls: 'He said that if it was not some brigadier or retired colonel, it was someone in a village who wanted to complain.

'I had to remind him that he was not the first guy who had tried to do such things to sport, to want to put a five-storey development on to a ground. I told him that the reason it would never be done at Chelsea is that there is a life in football that will never die.

'Much later, I had another meeting with Duggan, when he shook his head and admitted that he should have listened to me in the first place.'

The fact that he did not meant that Duggan went head to head with Bates. There was only ever going to be one winner and there was more passion and determination in Bates than Duggan had ever experienced in the world of big business. Here was an opponent who never gave up, never. The same rules applied to Harding. 'If I beat Duggan then I know I can beat anyone,' said Bates.

Mellor says, 'I never thought that Ken would cave in, not once did that cross my mind. Ken is a tough nut, and I say that approvingly. He can be equally tough in other ways. He is certainly a strong and opinionated man, who can be unreasonable. But, essentially, I always felt that he would win through.

'I have to admit, though, that I never thought he would get us this far. He always said that he wanted to make Chelsea the best club side in Europe. Well, he is nearing that goal. We, his supporters, always wondered if it would be possible. We should never have doubted how high he could take the club.

'Ken, in many ways, is a complicated man, but in terms of what he wants out of life he is quite straightforward. He always wanted a big position in football. Having settled at Chelsea it became his life. He wanted to create something special. It is not just about football now, it is about Chelsea

Village and everything that goes with that – the public involvement, the restaurants, hotels and penthouses. He has so many other plans for it.

'It is far more than a football club. It has become a community. In the eighties, he knew what he wanted to achieve, but cursed the people who wanted to stop him.

'There were times when I asked myself if he could pull it off. I thought he might die in the attempt. But never once did I believe that Ken Bates would sell out. Never once would he sell his soul to the property men. No way. Say what you like about him, but he fought tooth and nail to keep Chelsea afloat, then fought to get the club where it is today.'

Mellor believes that the economic cycle also helped Bates to do what he wanted. He says, 'We were fighting off Duggan and the property developers until such time when the potency of the property market fell. It got so bad for them that they headed down the tubes.' Duggan's company was one that suffered and the Royal Bank of Scotland had to move in. Unlike Duggan, they had no stomach for a fight and no inclination to take the ground away from Chelsea.

Bates and Chelsea finally exercised their option to buy the ground on 6 August 1988. It was a sweet, significant moment for Bates. A real battle won. Duggan had finally been kicked aside. 'The people who wanted Chelsea to go were left punching an empty shell,' says Bates. 'It annoyed me that they came in the first place. I had said to them that if they accepted that Chelsea were going to stay at Stamford Bridge, I would work with them.

'But they wouldn't listen. They wouldn't co-operate. So they had to be deflated. It was like a war. Two enemies with a line down the middle. And they bloody well were not going to get what was mine, or, more importantly, what belonged to the good people of Chelsea, the fans.'

One man who picked up the facts, figures and the whole story of the first ten years of Bates's reign was solicitor Mark Taylor. He now has his finger on the pulse of Chelsea's lifeblood and he says he can hardly believe what went on as Bates fought to keep Chelsea afloat.

'It was a long hard battle for Ken,' says Taylor, 'and it is easy now to look back and reflect without doing real justice to the effort he sustained. Basically, when Ken took control in 1982, the Mears family had sold the freehold of the company to property developers Marlar Estates. They granted SB Property Company – that is the Stamford Bridge Property Company – a seven-year lease, which expired in 1989.

'They then had a right to buy the ground if Cabra, which had taken over Marlar's interest, wanted to redevelop. And, during the lease, Cabra did get permission to redevelop. It was right at the top of the property market, so it seemed the only way Chelsea could stay at Stamford Bridge was to buy the ground.

'At first, the price could not be agreed, so it went to arbitration. Then the property market collapsed, which, of course, was in Chelsea's favour. Cabra were in a difficult position. They had borrowed the money on the site, as it was to be redeveloped. But the valuation of the site had fallen and there was no point in carrying on if the market had changed so dramatically.

'So, from wanting Chelsea out, they now wanted Chelsea to stay because, effectively, Chelsea were the only occupiers. But, of course, they wanted the best price.

'Eventually Cabra went bust and the Royal Bank of Scotland were left being owed a phenomenal amount of money. The bank did a deal with Chelsea whereby a subsidiary of the bank bought the ground and granted Chelsea a lease with the option of buying the ground completely within twenty years.

'There is no question that, on many occasions, Ken was on the verge of being kicked out. Realistically, it was the Mears who were responsible. The stand they built became so over-budget that it brought the club to its knees. They did not insist on a fixed price contract and the cost spiralled. It got delayed because of inflation and the club were dragged down as the cost of the stand slowly went up.

'The decision to build that stand was taken in 1972, when Chelsea was the bee's knees. But the team went downhill quickly and they were eventually relegated. Players were not replaced and the stand became the white elephant stand. It became a millstone around the club's neck.

'The club got in such a mess that the only way they could get their heads above water was to sell the freehold of the site. So Mears sold out.

'There is absolutely no doubt that if there had not been a man as tenacious as Ken Bates taking control then Chelsea would have folded.

'I have reviewed all the papers. Ken had lost the litigation but, because he was so strong willed, he continued to apply pressure on Cabra. A lot of others would have thrown in the towel and done what Cabra wanted him to.

'I believe he fought hard for three reasons. One, he began to love Chelsea – he certainly does now. Two, he hates being turned over – Cabra tried continuously, and that made him even stronger. Three, he knew what he wanted in the future for the club and that, in a way, kept him going more than anything else.'

No one who knows him, or who has worked with him, will be surprised that he won. Right at the start, this extraordinary man made it very clear that he knew what he wanted. Oldham were at one stage vulnerable, and available, and they cried out for someone with money. Bates had money. He also had amazing powers of inner strength and a ruthless streak that was determined to get to the top.

At his first board meeting at Oldham he produced a typed blueprint for the future. He told the directors that this was the plan and they could live with it, or lump it – or, indeed, get out. One director, a schoolmaster called Eric Beard, recalls, 'There was a pile of correspondence on the table at that first meeting. Bates looked at it, looked up and said, "I'll show you what to do with this," and he screwed it up and threw it on the floor.'

He was starting afresh. If Oldham were to flourish then it would be by his rules. He has applied the same principles ever since.

He admitted that he was in a hurry, and within a week he had met and hired former Burnley player Jimmy McIlroy.

McIlroy says, 'We met at a New Year's Eve party. I liked him straight away. He asked if I would like to be manager and I agreed immediately.

'He was a marvellous man with figures. He and the other directors would look at the balance sheet and Ken would let the others ramble on. Then he would pick up his pencil and start doing his alterations and calculations. I loved to see how the other directors' faces altered.

'He could turn a deficit of £50,000 into a profit of £100,000, no problem. He had the directors eating out of his hand. They would leave the meeting chuckling, saying, "We are quite well off." He had that gift.'

Bates began his first annual meeting at Oldham by standing up and blowing a whistle. Kickoff. Let battle commence. It has never been dull.

And he is still going, as fast and determined as ever. Ken Bates remains in the fast lane. There are those, not just in the past, but in football now, who don't know how he does it. It is not just the future of Chelsea he fought so hard for, and continues so to do. There are so many other characters and situations in football who have come up against him – and lost.

5 'You Don't Like Me? I Couldn't Care Less'

THE HARDER KEN BATES FOUGHT to keep Chelsea alive, the more his reputation grew. He has been called controversial ever since he opened his mouth, although he denies that he loses his temper. 'I do not rampage, scream, shout or make outrageous statements,' he says. 'I sometimes wonder at the headlines I get and the treatment I receive in the media. All I do is speak my mind. If I am asked a question, I answer it fairly. I say what I feel. If that upsets people, tough.'

And how he has upset people down the years. No one has escaped if they have dared to cross this man behind the mouth. The Football Association, the Professional Footballers' Association, other clubs, managers, the media, television, individual journalists, MPs, you name them, they have all fallen foul of the Bates tongue.

Feathers were ruffled the moment he walked into Stamford Bridge. All complimentary tickets for the staff were stopped. He followed this by putting up the price of watching Chelsea and told fans, 'This club was bankrupt and I have saved it. If the fans want First Division football here, they have got to pay for it.

'The supporters have been undercharged in the past. Prices have not gone up for two years and Chelsea have been losing £15,000 a home game. Many Chelsea fans have told me that if I am prepared to put my money where my mouth is, then so are they. It costs millions to run this club and we have got to balance the books. I do not believe our fans are broke.'

The players did not escape either. After just 6,903 supporters turned up to watch a laboured win over Bolton in December 1992 he told the playing staff, 'If you are not prepared to sweat blood for this club then you know where the door is.

'Every player at this club is playing for his and Chelsea's future. We will get rid of nine players at the end of this season. At the moment we have a pool of twenty-five and I believe that only Liverpool have more.

'These players have been earning far too much and giving back far too little. They have been isolated from the real world. They live in the stockbroker belt, drive expensive cars and do not seem to realise that many of their own suppporters are on the dole.'

Bates took rapid action bringing the supporters closer to the club. He sent out invitations to box holders and executive members for a meeting to discuss the future. There was also a questionnaire in the programme allowing terrace supporters to give their point of view. Bates said at the time, 'There is no point in wasting time. It is important from my point of view to find out what the real Chelsea fans want. Their opinions are important to me in finding out where the problems lie and also for developing future policies.'

Bates also met the players for an open forum. There were question and answer sessions with no holds barred. 'They knew who I was and it was important for everyone to get to know me. At that stage I was the new owner, nothing else. I had to get closer to the people who kept this club afloat, the fans and the players.'

It was a master stroke. Ever since those early days, Bates has had the Chelsea fans on his side. Even at the height of the Harding war, they never once turned against him. When Bates banished Harding to the stand for a home match against Spurs, Harding and the police feared crowd trouble. There was not a sniff of unrest. Not one supporter turned against Bates, not one show of public demonstration against him.

Chelsea fans have good, long memories. They know that without Bates, old grey beard, there would be no fairy tale and no club to support. 'I have always been proud of my relationship with the supporters. They know that deep down I am with them, even if I do not always show it,' he says. 'When I look back now I have no regrets about what I did or how I handled it. I have done things at all times because I thought they were necessary. I hope people now realise that they were.'

Racism was another big headache he had to overcome in those early days, and he did it in the style that only Bates knows. There had been a lot of bad feeling on the Stamford Bridge terraces in the eighties but Bates answered that with, 'If a three-legged, one-eyed Muslim Red Indian is our best striker and can help us back into the First Division, then he will be in the team.'

Bates has received letters from supporters deploring the use of black players, and also from fans deploring the racial abuse. In March 1983, he was sent a booby-trapped letter filled with razor blades and containing the message, 'No more blacks at Chelsea.' Former secretary Sheila Marson opened the letter and almost had her fingers sliced by eight blades. She says, 'It was pure luck that saved me. For some reason I opened the letter along the side and not the top, and I saw the blades.' At that stage Chelsea had only one black player in their first-team squad, Paul Canoville.

The other major problem was hooligans and their terrace violence. Chelsea had their share of scum support and Bates walked a tightrope of defending the good Chelsea fan and denouncing the idiots. There were ugly scenes at Derby, Brighton and at Stamford Bridge.

On more than one occasion Bates went on to the pitch to try to appease the heaving mass, calling for truce and sense. He often blamed the media for their handling of the club and their treatment of the hooligan problem at Chelsea. After one riot at Derby, where fans and police were hurt, and seats ripped up and thrown on to the pitch, Bates turned on the media. He said, 'I will say it rather bitterly – you have got what you have been waiting for. This game has had a bigger build-up than a Joe Bugner title fight. But it was almost an anti-climax for you.

'I do not deny that there is a hooligan problem at Stamford Bridge. After all, why should Chelsea be any different to

Milwall, Spurs, West Ham, Manchester United, Liverpool, Portsmouth, Newcastle . . . shall I go on?

'What differs is the press treatment of Chelsea. We are the only club constantly criticised, consistently persecuted and emphasised. If Chelsea has the worst reputation in the country it is because of irresponsible reporting.'

And he meant it. From those bitter words came non-stop attacks on the media in his now infamous match programme notes. 'If you are big enough to say it, you have to be big enough to take it,' he says now.

Bates even put an undercover plot into operation in an effort to flush out the troublemakers. A team of private detectives mixed with supporters on match days with orders to report back to the chairman. At around the same time, the government produced its own working-party report and it got an immediate blast from Bates. He said, 'Thirteen people from four different departments produced this report. I suppose they thought it was better than working. But what a pity that they didn't ask one football person. The suggestion that there should be a league table based on their hooligan record is ridiculous. Will they hold the final at Wembley for the top two? What will happen if fans don't like being bottom? Will they go out and kick a few more heads to move up the league?'

Bates was one of the first to advocate the use of closed-circuit TV cameras at football stadiums to identify the hooligans. 'It was obvious to me,' he now says. 'I like to think I have been ahead of the game on and off the pitch.'

There was never a dull moment. At the end of 1983, he announced that, for the first time since 1971, the club were in the black. 'Chelsea are solvent,' he said. 'We can even let the manager have some money for players.'

But just a few months later, more problems were to happen with the old regime. He discovered they were still trying to do deals behind his back. In January 1984, he had to make a dash across London to get an injunction delaying the sale of Stamford Bridge. Then he raced to a Knightsbridge hotel where the injunctions were served preventing directors of SB Property Company transferring their shares to Marlar Estates, who wanted to redevelop the ground.

Had Bates not succeeded then Chelsea would have been forced to ground-share. 'It was that close,' he recalls. The Knightsbridge meeting had just ended when Bates rushed in. Viscount Chelsea, one of the men involved with the sale, was discussing his love of football when Bates handed him a writ. Just another battle, just another day in the life of chairman Ken. 'Just another winning day,' he corrects.

When you consider that Bates was not only fighting off those who wanted to kill the club, but also that he was fighting a massive hooligan problem, then you can only admire his commitment. Football was then an era of terrace fighting and fences at stadiums.

In April 1985, and without getting permission from the FA or the London Council, Bates erected a high fence around parts of Stamford Bridge, topped with electric wiring.

Bates thought of the idea on one of his early-morning strolls around his farm. If electric fences can keep cows in, it can bloody well keep in hooligans, he thought to himself. The idea was met with horror by the authorities and Bates, typically, hit back hard. 'There will be a single strand of electric wire, the type that controls cows.

'It will be above three strands of barbed wire and will be eleven feet above the ground. We do not intend to keep on building higher fences and we think this is the ultimate deterrent. People may howl about it being dangerous but it has been used in farming for a long time.

'If you touch it you will get a shock which will make you shoot off it. There will be appropriate warning signs around the ground. I expect the majority of fans, who are law abiding citizens, will be one hundred per cent behind it.'

It was Bates's response to the FA ordering clubs to erect bigger and better fences following crowd trouble at a Milk Cup tie between Chelsea and Sunderland. 'Serious crimes warrant serious punishment. Mrs Thatcher came to power on a law and order platform. Both with the miners and in the Falklands she has demonstrated her will to win battles of her choosing. So far there is no evidence that there is a political will to tackle a serious problem that is affecting a lot of people.'

There were many calls for Chelsea to be banned, closed down and heavily punished as hooliganism continued to follow them around. Bates blamed too much media attention, fought it in his own way and turned on the media whenever they dared to suggest that he was not doing enough.

After one call, this time from Jeff Powell of the *Daily Mail*, for Chelsea's punishment to fit the crimes of their fans, Bates produced this reply. He said, 'The trouble at Chelsea on Monday gave the media a great opportunity to focus on a serious problem that is growing due to the indifference of the authorities.

'There is no simple, easy solution to soccer violence. If there were, there would be no problem. It cannot be viewed in isolation as it reflects the society in which we live.

'Violence in society was once mainly linked with robbery or drink. Today, it has evolved through a means – political and industrial strife – to a degenerate end, as evidenced by the battering of penniless pensioners and the ritual murder of complete strangers.

'If shutting Chelsea solved the hooligan problem, I would do it tomorrow, but it wouldn't.

'The heads buried in the sand do not include mine. They belong to those people who suggest the problem is confined to Chelsea, an impression encouraged by others in the game who are happy to sweep their own trouble under the carpet, hoping that it goes away.

'The serious problems at Ipswich and Norwich were not reported at such length, and there is violence at most other large clubs which does not receive the same exposure as Chelsea.

'This is stupid because until the full significance of the situation is recognised, the government will not act.

'There is evidence that trouble at London grounds is fermented by a hard core who pick their matches and plan para-military fashion. Their presence reinforces the local morons. Most of the lemmings who follow them cause little trouble. Eliminate the hard core and much will be solved.

'The police have a squad for drugs and murder. We need a

hooligan squad to take the initiative instead of reacting to trouble afterwards.

'Last October, I wrote to the commissioner of the Metropolitan Police to request an urgent meeting to submit my ideas for tackling the problem – it was refused.

'Meanwhile, although Chelsea's relations with their local force are good, match days are sometimes chaos because we are constantly sent police who are unfamiliar with the ground.

'Soccer and the press should also work together more closely. A serious investigative campaign by Fleet Street would identify and expose the root cause in great detail. The power of the press would force the government to take action.

'A groundswell of public opinion would force the authorities to face up to their responsibilities towards the overwhelming majority of people who are sickened by the cancer of violence in society.

'The problems of a tax system that subsidises excessive transfer fees yet penalises ground improvements is compounded by the fact that money is drained from the game by the government.

'Chelsea have done a great deal already. We have banned alcohol on away trains, built perimeter fences and a family enclosure, installed closed circuit TV and established our own supporters' club with preferential treatment for members.

'The urgent improvements needed include better access to ease congestion in surrounding streets, direct links to the tube and British Rail lines, increased car parking, covered accommodation, complete segregation of supporters, better toilets and a social centre where people can be made to feel an integral part of the club.

'But these must wait until Chelsea's pursuit of the freehold of the Stamford Bridge site is successfully concluded.

'Meanwhile, the club tackles its problem at the present poorly designed ground with a hard-working staff learning from mistakes. I wish Jeff Powell had dealt more with these issues and less with abusing me personally.

'I work six days a week for the club, gratis, because I love football, which has given Powell a good living for many years.

He has a responsibility to help the game from which he has had so much. If not, perhaps he should take the advice he gave me and retire from the scene . . . at least for the time being.'

This was typical Bates, taking on all-comers. 'But I never lost my temper,' he emphasises. 'It was never Blaster Bates.'

The fence was never turned on, either. Would he have done it? 'If there had been a way, I would have turned it on.'

It rankled with Bates that he stoutly defended the GLC's right to exist only for the council not to back him at the eleventh hour. He snapped, 'The dafties at the GLC have now cast themselves as the pro-hooligan, anti-football supporter. I once went to the House of Commons for a debate with MPs on football hooliganism. Do you know how many MPs were there? Three. That is why I do not take the views of these people seriously.'

His criticism of Powell all those years ago was only the start of a running battle with the media. He has fallen out with many of us over the years and others have appeared in his programme notes, a column that has become notorious for its often vicious handling of situations.

My own view is that Bates loves the media. He enjoys the crack, the publicity, the company and the lunches, even if relationships falter when the criticism of him or his club is high. Harry Harris of the *Daily Mirror* is a classic example of Bates's Jekyll and Hyde relationship with the media. Bates and Harris once fell out big time, with Bates winning a libel case against Harris and the *Mirror* and then proudly buying himself a new Bentley with the proceeds.

Such was his contempt for Harris that he called the men's toilet after him in the club's press room underneath the main stand. The Harry Harris Memorial Toilet.

Then came the Harding bust up, carried as we know through the tabloids, and Harris sided with Bates. He was back on-side and repaid for his loyalty with a stream of information. At that time, Bates needed Harris as much as Harris needed him. There is nothing wrong with that, journalism is a tough world and you get what you can get.

But then Harris became close to Ruud Gullit, via his London

agent, Jon Smith, and when Gullit and Chelsea parted company there was a clear dilemma for him. Harris did not once criticise Gullit, even though Bates and Chelsea condemned him for being too greedy and published his full demands. The *Mirror*'s story said instead, 'Bridge of Lies. Who is telling the truth?' Another interesting twist is that Harris has since written Gullit's autobiography in which he talks about Chelsea and all that he felt was wrong with it.

Bates, as we know, insists on loyalty. It is important to him. Gullit is now out of his thoughts. The man is no longer important to Chelsea. He will not take kindly to any criticism from him towards the club, especially after giving Gullit his first job in management. He is also now disappointed with Harris, someone he thought of as being completely on his side.

Bates calls his relationship with the press an 'anti-love affair' and partly places the blame for this on a club decision to put the press box on the opposite side of the stadium, above the stand in the old TV gantry. Bates says, 'It was a former secretary, Sheila Marson, who came up with the idea of putting the press box in the TV gantry. I have been blamed ever since, but it was never my idea.

'We spent a fortune on tarting it up, with glass on the front and a bar. The Football Writers' Association were not happy and Steve Curry, then of the *Daily Express*, had an appointment to come and see me. He cancelled at the last minute and never showed up again. Then, on the first day of the season, there were complaints, but I told them that it was too late.

'Curry said that he had sent me a letter complaining about the facilities. He did, but it was dated May and postmarked August. He had forgotten to post it. So much for the caring FWA. I have been slagged off in the media ever since.'

More rows followed, but not always with the media. There was a massive bust up with Luton Town and their then chairman, David Evans. The bust up began when Luton banned all away supporters from their Kenilworth Road ground. Bates reacted by giving his boardroom passes and directors' box seats to fans. 'Why should I go?' said Bates.

'They should be playing in the Vauxhall League. That is where little clubs belong.'

He had more run-ins with the TV people and the FA before introducing a Save the Bridge fund, a scheme to raise money to help keep Chelsea at Stamford Bridge. The money raised is said to have gone on legal fees to maintain the fight against property developers and other official wranglings.

And Bates kept fighting. In the late eighties there came a twist with the chairman attempting to warn off the property developers from buying the club's site. Bates paid £725 to place a full-page advertisement in the Estate Agents' Gazette. The advertisement, placed by an unnamed estate agent on behalf of Mr Bates, stated: 'The Chelsea Football and Athletic Company are lessees of the land and premises known as Stamford Bridge Football and Athletic Grounds by a lease dated August 19, 1982.

'Under the terms of this lease Chelsea held an option to purchase the freehold of the estate, such an option becoming exercisable on or after August 19, 1988. At no time has Chelsea undertaken or indicated that it will not be exercising that option.'

It was Bates putting the frighteners on. But Marlar Estates counter-claimed by saying that in six years of wheeling and dealing, since Bates bought the club, he had not produced an offer acceptable to Marlar for the purchase of this prime site, which was then valued at somewhere between £60 million and £100 million.

Bates was up against it, especially as Marlar had put the site up for sale with London estate agents Savills. Marlar also had planning permission on the ground. Bates's reaction was typical. 'Sod them. They'll not win and I fight on,' he cursed.

It has been the story of his life. One long fight. People have listened to him, some have acted, others have dismissed him as a dreamer. Marlar were no different to the others.

Back in 1966, when he was chairman of Oldham, Bates wrote an article for the Football League Review. In it he said that football in England is sold far too cheaply. He said, 'No business can run efficiently when management is obsessed by money worries, as ninety per cent of the league clubs in the country are.

'I feel steps should be taken to educate the public to the fact that they must pay economic prices for their football if they are to have the standard of play and improved ground facilities that everybody requires.

'Many clubs fail to take advantage of their supporters' good will. These people are perfectly willing to spend more money at a football match if the facilities are available. But at so many grounds you cannot find the programme seller and the places for refreshments are so remote and antiquated, and the quality of the fare offered so poor, that one is not encouraged to take advantage of them.

'In the close season we re-seated our main stand, installed modern tip-up seats and provided luxury boxes where football can be watched in warm and dry comfort. The dismal Johnnies forecast that these would be unsuccessful but they were sold out before completion and we already have a waiting list for next season.

'In my opinion, supporters are prepared to pay the price involved for better facilities and we are working on plans to provide Boundary Park with increased seating, better refreshment bars, sited strategically around the ground, improved facilities for drinking and a high standard of pre-match entertainment to encourage the fans to come early.'

So, all those years ago, Bates was planning and thinking far quicker than the game itself and, most significantly, the people who ran it. But he knew what he wanted. If Oldham could not give him what he wanted then Chelsea could. He would build his dream club and no one was going to stop him.

He says, 'You cannot stand still and I never have. People don't like me, I know that. I couldn't care less.

'I have fought hard for what I have got, for what is mine. No one is going to take this away from me or the club's fans.'

And fight on he did. That battle with Marlar was in July 1988. He resisted for another four years, refusing to be beaten. It was taken to the wire before the final breakthrough that he had waited for. When it came, it was one of the sweetest moments of his Chelsea career.

He will certainly never forget the day. It was the moment he finally won control of Stamford Bridge – the site, as well as the Football Club.

6 The First Vital Victory

I T WAS ABOUT 7.30 p.m. on the evening of 15 December 1992 and Ken Bates was driving home in his Bentley. The cassette player filled the car with classical music and he felt relaxed. The phone jolted him from his concentration and a voice at the other end of the line said, 'We have just completed, Mr Bates. Have a nice evening.'

The voice was that of director Yvonne Todd, one of Bates's trusted aides and someone who has been with the chairman all the way through. She had just given Bates the news he had waited ten years to hear.

The freehold of Stamford Bridge was finally in his hands. No more property developers, no more threats. Now, at last, he could go ahead with his Chelsea dream. And finish it without any more aggravation.

Bates says, 'It was one of the highlights, if not the highlight, of this long fight. I had been at a meeting since ten and left it at seven. I was confident that the deal would be done and left them to complete the finishing touches.

'The phone call confirmed what I expected but it was still great to get the news from Yvonne. I was on my way to celebrate anyway, but confirmation made it an evening to remember.

'Ten years is a long time. But in that split second so much rushed by. The fights, the threats, the meetings, the money spent, everything. It was as if it had been minutes instead of a decade. Ten years out of my life. Relief? Yes, definitely.

'I don't care what anyone says about me. I kept my promise. I said from day one that Chelsea would not leave Stamford Bridge and that phone call confirmed it. When I walked through the door for the first time I saw what I wanted from this club. I didn't realise it would take so long because I didn't realise that Chelsea were in such a mess.

'But I knew that night in 1992 that anything was possible. I knew that from that moment Chelsea could, and would, become the greatest club side in Britain. It was a bloody good Christmas.'

Bates, of course, had plotted and planned the capture of the freehold. He knew that without it there would be no hotels, restaurants, penthouses, future . . . nothing. That was not the dream.

A year earlier he had formed Chelsea Village, a holding company which had various subsidiaries.

He took advice from lawyers, the FA and everyone he believed would help him. He had many conversations with the Royal Bank of Scotland, the bankers who had taken the lease from Cabra when they got into financial difficulty. The Royal Bank of Scotland, as we have said, never wanted to see Chelsea leave Stamford Bridge. They were keen to do a deal. It was just a question of when Bates could do it.

Success came at that meeting with the bank and, of course, it had been requested and plotted by Bates. He says, 'I don't think people realise just how much went on or, indeed, just what goes on behind the scenes. This was not just another meeting. We had waited ten years for it, planned it throughout.'

Although a lot of people thought Bates had bought the lease in 1992, this was not the case. What Bates did was to obtain the lease from the bank with an option to purchase it for £16.5 million at anytime within twenty years. Mark Taylor says, 'It was a huge breakthrough because, for the first time, Chelsea owned everything. The club, the site and the freehold. Ken knew that £16.5 million would not be worth so much in twenty years' time. It was a massive comfort to get it and once again the club can be thankful to him for securing it. After that meeting Chelsea knew they had at least twenty years' security.'

Typical of Bates, it took him just five years to purchase the freehold from the bank. Always a man in a hurry, he negotiated the £16.5 million purchase after Chelsea had completed their Euro-bond deal in December 1997. Bates says: 'It is amazing how much has happened in December. I wonder what will be next.'

The Euro-bond was another huge breakthrough. Bates, always a man for perfect timing, completed it on his 66th birthday. 'What a marvellous present,' he chuckled. 'The dream is now a reality.'

The deal, a ten-year bond with SBC Warburg Dillon Read, is essentially a method of borrowing a large sum of money. Chelsea borrowed £75 million. The financiers seek a group of investors and offer them part of the deal.

It allowed Chelsea to consolidate their debts by paying an annual interest of 8.72 per cent of the bond's value to the financiers – around £6 million. But it did represent a substantial saving on their previous situation, in which they were repaying separate loans from the banks at interest rates of between 9.5 and 10 per cent.

Chelsea do not have to repay the bond until December 2007 and the £6 million annual interest will not be difficult because each Premiership club receives around £8 million from the new television deal with Sky and the BBC. There will also be a major positive cash flow for the club because the Euro-bond money allows return from the self-financing and profit-making ventures such as the hotels, flats and leisure complex.

Bates says, 'It was a massive situation for the club, a real turning point. There were those who said that no one would invest in Chelsea once Matthew Harding had died, or that there would be no investment because of Ken Bates. I think that ended that nonsense once and for all.

'It was a marvellous moment for me because it allowed us to move up, to slip into another gear and become part of the elite.'

It was also the last uncertainty out of the way and meant that the club were no longer beholden to the Harding estate. Bates had rid himself, at last, of everything to do with Harding. 'I did it for Chelsea and the future, nothing else,' he insisted.

Harding, of course, had bought the freehold of the ground when he had battled so hard to de-throne Bates and gain control of the club. Ownership passed to his estate when he died but the Euro-bond deal allowed Bates to buy it for £11.6 million. The rest of the money was ploughed into completing the Village.

Mark Taylor has no doubt about the importance of the Euro-deal. He says, 'It was an amazing deal, especially when you consider that Newcastle had tried to do something similar a month before and failed.

'It is basically a loan and you sell proportions to various people. All the institutions that bought ours were pukka institutions. It's safe to say that everything is now safe in the hands of Chelsea Village.

'I remember the day well, 17 December 1997 – five years and two days after we had secured the ground.

'It is the second most important deal Chelsea have ever done. The first was in 1992 when we first secured the ground.

'The Euro-bond deal means that the money is in place for everything – an annexe to the hotel, completion of the West Stand, a sport and leisure centre, an entrance to Stamford Bridge, anything, the money is all there.

'I can still see Ken in 1992 showing me a model of the Stamford Bridge he wanted. I thought then that he was in dreamland. But, five years later, it was there. It is an amazing story. He is an amazing man.'

The public flotation was Bates's idea. He knew that he could not float a football club because you cannot pay dividends on a football club. After getting clearances from the Revenue and FA he formed Chelsea Village.

It is Chelsea Village that runs the whole thing. And each subsidiary has a managing director. For instance, the football club's managing director is Colin Hutchinson, a man Bates brought in from Wimbledon to help him run the Save the Bridge fund. Hutchinson has become one of the most respected football administrators in the country, working closely with the Chelsea manager and reporting to the Chelsea Village directors.

It is the Village that runs the whole show and all the shares in the football club are owned by the Village. The football club is a subsidiary of the Village with Bates owning 30 million of the shares, about 22 per cent of the issued capital. Bates is chairman of both Chelsea Village and Chelsea Football Club.

Mark Taylor says: 'A big shareholder in an investment trust in Guernsey, invested in Chelsea Village early on when we needed money. We bought that building at the front of Stamford Bridge then to block Cabra's development plans. If we owned the front of the Fulham Road it would be difficult for them to develop the rest of the ground because they would not have the access they needed.'

All master plans, plots and deals from the mind of Bates. The active mind of a man who knew what he wanted in 1982 and bloody well refused to let anyone stop him. But they still tried, even after he had gone so far down the line to securing his dream, even after Harding's death.

Bates talks openly about the situations but dismisses them in his own quest for getting to the very top with Chelsea. It is rather like swatting a fly with Ken. These people come into his life and he biffs them around before they fly out again. Harrods owner Mohammed Al Fayed was treated in exactly the same way.

Bates says. 'The only time I ever offered to sell out was during the Harding saga when, as a tactical ploy, I challenged him to put up or shut up. I never was going to sell out, anyway. He did the latter. He shut up.

'Later, I was introduced to the McCarthy brothers who are partners of Richard Branson. They discussed taking up a minority stake by subscribing for the unissued shares but talks broke down when it became clear that they wanted control, which was not on the table. I was not having that.

'When Rune Hauge introduced me to the Norwegians, who have subsequently got involved with Wimbledon, they too wanted too much for too little.' Bates could not believe how many people came out of the woodwork to challenge him, especially after he had won the major battles. His attitude was this: I have done the hard work and now you want the glory. You can all fuck off.

'The Harrods saga was somewhat different,' Bates continues. 'John MacArthur was a financial advisor who helped Chelsea when we were battling for the ground in 1992. He was also working for the Al Fayeds and MacArthur introduced me to the elder brother. We ate smoked salmon and drank champagne at his penthouse flat, discussed the deal to finance the ground purchase and shook hands on the deal.

'Unfortunately, it later transpired that it meant nothing and no deal was forthcoming.

'Then, around November 1996, Al Fayed was offered Watford. The club didn't interest him, so he got MacArthur to contact me again. We met and discussed the idea of him taking a substantial minority stake in Chelsea. He visited Stamford Bridge, liked what he saw and invited me to Harrods where we lunched in the Georgian restaurant. So far so good.

'We discussed gross selling, using the purchasing power for Chelsea's benefit. I even suggested that it could be called Harrods Chelsea Village. Mohammed was careful not to shake hands but instructed MacArthur to do the deal. Michael Cole showed me around Harrods and I returned to Stamford Bridge.

'All very nice. Then the delays started. Meanwhile, they approached the Harding trustees to buy their stake, but only if I would sell mine. No deal. End of story.

'Subsequently they decided they were lifelong Fulham supporters. Still, something came out of it – they are building a Harrods Village just down the road from Craven Cottage. He must have taken my advice.'

Mark Taylor spent four days solid with Al Fayed's people, thrashing out a deal. 'We were approached by Al Fayed,' he explained. 'He said that he wanted to acquire a stake in the club. Chelsea did have unissued capital. For instance, everyone knows that the trustees of Matthew Harding's estate would like to flog it.

'After four days we had got to the stage when a deal could be done. A document was prepared. Then, at the last minute, he said that he wanted a seat on the board as well as a twenty-five per cent stake. He then said that Chelsea should go private and told Ken to make an offer to buy all his shares back.'

Bates's reaction was typical. He told Al Fayed's advisors that it had taken him almost twenty fucking years to make it a public company and he was not going to take it back now.

It was the same old story for Bates. People were trying to override him. 'It's amazing that they didn't realise how strong he was or how much he cared about the club,' adds Taylor. Ken wants the people to have a slice of Chelsea. What Al Fayed wanted was to control it, like he is doing at Fulham.

'He knew that Chelsea would have saved him ten years. He will probably get Fulham into the First Division easily enough but it is the next step, the Premiership, that is hard. And then to sustain it, and then to grow big.

'Chelsea are big. Ken Bates has got us a hell of a long way quickly and, clearly, there are envious eyes. Al Fayed did not annoy him. People are coming in all the time, wanting to acquire stakes in the club.'

Peter Middleton did annoy him. Bates sniffed him out quickly and got rid of him. Taylor says, 'Middleton is chief executive of Solomon Brothers, a huge investment bank in the City. He came on board soon after Harding died.

'He likes a high profile and being chairman of Chelsea PLC would have suited him very nicely.

'It got to the stage when we had to tell him that, as a board, we were as one behind Ken. We said that it was the board who appointed the chairman and not the shareholders.'

It got to the stage when the directors told Middleton to put up or shut up. A special board meeting was called with the Middleton situation on top of the agenda. Taylor recalls, 'Peter just walked in, threw his passes down on to the table, said 'See you' and walked out. That was it.

'Middleton was not realistic. Ken has put a lot of his life into Chelsea. How did Peter think he could just walk in and take over?' Another enemy gone. As Bates says, 'Another johnny-come-lately out of the way.'

Bates now simply wants to get on with his life. He wants to complete the Chelsea dream and sit and watch the best team in England win the Championship. Why, at his age, should he put up with people he does not like, respect or get on with? 'I am,' he adds, 'quite a straightforward person. If you ask me a question, I will give you an answer, my thoughts. I am not bland, that is certain, but I do not believe I am controversial either. Some people get to the top by playing the party line. I am where I am by working hard and being honest with people. I am not a celebrity but people do seem to like to talk to me.'

He recalls a recent New Year's Eve when he and Suzannah were at an expensive dinner-dance – black ties, speeches, the lot. 'I had only sat down for a few minutes when about seven people converged on me asking why this and why that. I did not need it. It was pressure on a social occasion and I did not need it.

'So we went home and saw the New Year in with cheese on toast and a bottle of champagne. I enjoyed it more.

'I have got to the stage in my life when I do not have to put up with situations I do not like. If people do not like my rules, tough.'

7 The Managers: John Neal to David Webb

I F THERE IS ONE THING that does upset Bates it is the suggestion that he has ruthlessly sacked all his managers. 'Prove it,' he says. Since 1982 he has had eight of them, starting with John Neal, who he inherited from the Mears regime, and running down John Hollins, Bobby Campbell, Ian Porterfield, David Webb, Glenn Hoddle, Ruud Gullit and now Gianluca Vialli. Bates says, 'The only one I didn't enjoy working with, the only real mistake I made, was Ian Porterfield.

'The others played their part in the development. Neal left because of ill health, Hollins was sacked, so was Porterfield, Campbell left by mutual consent, Webby was never promised the job after helping us stay in the First Division, Hoddle went to manage England, Gullit would not sign a contract and now there is Vialli.

'I deny strongly that I am the ruthless baron who rides roughshod over his managers. Ask any of them. I don't pick the team or refuse them money to buy the players. What I do is run the club. I delegate, and those people report back to me. If there is something going wrong, I want to know about it, and if it needs correcting, I correct it, along with others I trust. End of story.

'I have only fired two managers in sixteen years, which isn't bad when you consider the pressures of football. We are not a club, I am not a person, who enjoys massive turnover on the playing side. Like anyone, I like stability. Chelsea need stability.

'We thought we had it with Hoddle and he defected. We thought we had it with Gullit, and he blew it. Now we have Vialli. In two years' time I do not want to hire anyone else, regardless of what people may say.'

Clearly, Bates has admiration and a warmth for Neal. Neal, the softly spoken Welshman, was in place when he walked into the club and the two men worked together, re-building on the pitch while Bates fought his battles. They went through a lot together. There were fall-outs and plenty of stories have been written and said about this relationship. The bottom line is that they enjoyed each other's company and Bates now even says, 'John Neal could still be at Chelsea today, had it not been for his illness [a heart by-pass operation]. He could have been a Sir Matt Busby figure to this club, someone who went from manager to director and then right upstairs to overlord the playing side. I have only respect for him.'

Neal calls Bates 'the old boy', a clear indication of the affection he holds for him. Neal took over at Stamford Bridge in April 1981, a year before the Bates era began. He was appointed when the combination of Geoff Hurst and Bobby Gould had to be replaced.

'When Ken took over I was very aware of the trouble the club was in,' recalls Neal. 'We had an awful team. A lot of people thought it was good, I know. So did he. We almost got relegated in his first season, finishing eighteenth in the old Second Division. It is the worst position I have ever been in during my career as a manager. Clive Walker scored a goal at Bolton to keep us afloat.

'Bates could have sacked me, I know that. He didn't and I will always be grateful for that. Mind you, he probably didn't have any money to pay me off. Eventually we proved great for each other.

'After that first season, he knew something had to be done. Under the old regime, the Mears, Sir Richard Attenborough, that lot, there had been no money available. So Ken set about creating some money. We got rid of a lot of the players. Some didn't want to go, others had their contracts bought out. Ken knew there had to be a turnover. That summer, we bought nine new players and just took off.

'I think we both knew the value of money. We shared an awareness that Chelsea needed at that stage.

'I sensed from the word go just how ambitious he was. He wanted the best for Chelsea and he would leave no stone unturned to get what he wanted. Yes, he was ruthless. He had to be.

'But now I can look back at leisure, and Ken Bates was undoubtedly the best chairman I ever worked with. He came with me to watch matches. We went all over the country together, especially when we were in the process of re-building the side.'

Chelsea fans will remember well the players Neal found and signed – with a little help from 'the old boy'. In came Kerry Dixon, David Speedie, Pat Nevin, Joey Jones, Joe McLaughlin, Eddie Niedzwiecki. 'I signed them all,' recalls Neal. 'People didn't realise just how good the side was.

'I got Speedie from Darlington, Dixon from Reading, Nevin, what a little gem he was, from Clyde. Then there was also Nigel Spackman. God, what a team it was. Ian McNeil was my scout and assistant and he went where angels fear to tread. He was a valuable servant of the club and helped us discover those players.

'We didn't mind signing those players whom others had failed to handle. Mickey Thomas was probably the best example. I had known him for years in Wales and knew that he could be the final piece of the jigsaw. I was delighted to sign him – he was perfect for the team.'

Chelsea won their first game of the season, 5–0 against the late Peter Taylor's Derby County, and they never looked back. Dixon got 28 goals, they won the League easily and Bates had begun to enjoy himself.

'Ken Bates was his own man and he knew I was too,' Neal adds. 'He knew I would do my own thing but, hands up, he supported me. Within two years the team had been transformed. With Ken as chairman all my energy could go on the team, he had all the other things on his mind.

'In the end he left the team totally to me. When he came into the dressing room before a game and I thought he was outstaying his welcome, I would just say to him, 'OK Ken, go on, piss off.' I told him that I would now try and undo the damage he had done with his comments to the players. It was banter, but firmly stated.'

The one thing that Bates and Neal did row about was the manager's addiction to smoking. 'He used to come into my office and complain about the smoke. It was the same every day,' adds Neal. It was a habit that was eventually to cost Neal his job.

Neal began to suffer heart problems during the 1983/84 season and eventually needed a by-pass operation. 'It didn't help me, or hinder me for that matter,' he says, 'although Bates worried about me.

'I was reluctant to change things. We were sixth in the First Division, the crowds were good and, for the first time, the club had a bit of money to spend on players. I could see a real rosy future for us.

'The chairman kept on about my condition. I was still working hard, travelling all over the country looking at players and opponents, and he said that he was worried, that he didn't want to be responsible for me killing myself. He wanted me to go upstairs in the boardroom and become a godfather looking over the playing side.

'The trouble is that when you're doing a job properly and being successful, you don't want to change things. Eventually, however, I agreed with him, little knowing that the move would be my downfall.

'I was no good upstairs. I hated it. I was, and always will be, a players' man. I loved being with the players. There I was, sitting upstairs watching someone else run my team – that was no good. There is no question that I would have stayed on as manager had Ken not suggested something different. You can't blame him. He was protecting me, even though – and I can admit this now – I was a useless director.'

The man Bates turned to was John Hollins, the England midfield player who had been a Chelsea legend but had been dropped by Neal. 'John got past it and had to be replaced,' Neal now explains. 'The other problem was that Ken thought

John was a better coach, a better man-manager, than he actually was.

'He attributed much of our success to John's coaching skills. However, the club's success was down to Ian and me, not John Hollins. What I had to then endure was watching Hollins destroy the team I had built. It could possibly have worked, with me as a consultant director and John and Ian running the team. But not once did he come to me for advice. Not once.

'I thought that John would want to build on what I had achieved, to use my principles. I thought he would have been sensible. He just ruined it instead.

'He found the change from player to coach and then to manager too difficult. I had the players' respect; he had to win it. As a coach you can sit on the fence, be everyone's friend, but you can't do that when you're the manager. You have to make decisions and use your man-management skills. Hollins, for instance, couldn't handle Mickey Thomas, who was such a valuable, important part of the team.

'It eventually had to end. Hollins was cocking it up, Bates was justifying his appointment . . . and I was in the background. I remember once watching the side play at QPR. We always won there, always beat Terry Venables, but Hollins changed the side and we got stuffed.

'Then we got stuffed at Cardiff and someone from the evening paper asked me what I thought of the team and my new position. I said I was disappointed. The article got twisted and twirled and was printed across the country. Bates played the big man and sacked me.

'It was the only thing that went sour on us. The parting began with my operation, increased with his concern and ended when I had to go into the boardroom. I was never happy there and our relationship was never the same.

'It's a shame because I felt that we started something, and we never really finished it. I do feel proud that Ken and I were together at the start of this dream he always spoke about. He talked to me about his ambitions for the club and, good luck to him, he has done it.'

Neal now spends his time playing golf (handicap eight) and

nursing his way through life. 'I have got away with this heart thing for years and as long as I have my golf I am happy.'

He returned to Stamford Bridge last year to attend an anniversary occasion. Gullit played in the game and he saw a lot of old faces. 'Most importantly,' he says. 'The crowd gave me a standing ovation.

'It was a moving moment for me. They had not forgotten and I will always treat it as an honour to manage such a big club. I had a great record there and a big picture of the day we won the Second Division Championship still hangs in my hall.

'I have not spoken to Ken Bates for some time. We have our memories. We went through a lot together. He was battling to hold on to the club and yet financing me.

'Ken Bates is an icon. He is Mr Chelsea. He is the club through and through. I have a lot of respect for the man. We had our ups and downs but we were our own men. We liked that in each other. Chelsea have not got where they are today without Ken Bates being his own man.'

Thomas was one of the players in at the start of Bates's dream. 'John Neal signed me in January 1984, from Stoke for £75,000,' he recalls. 'I met him on the M1 at Watford Gap. Yes, it is one of those signings you hear about. A real cloak and dagger job. I was signed with the manager saying, "See me on junction whatever."

'I had almost signed eighteen months before, when Neal asked me to talk to Bates. We spoke at 11.30 one night and he admitted that Neal wanted me, but he didn't. He had heard all about my bad-boy reputation and had been told not to touch me. But he was backing his manager and told me to meet him at the Manchester Piccadilly Hotel the next day.

'When I put the phone down I thought, Sod that, I'm not signing for him. Ken was driving up to Manchester the next day when he heard that I had signed for someone else. I didn't like what he said about me and thought that there is no way I could play for a chairman like that.'

Neal eventually got his man when Thomas changed his mind later on. 'I walked into a great side. There was Dixon, Speedie, Jones, John Bumstead, who was very underrated, Spackman,

Nevin – it was top class and we went from strength to strength. I scored twice on my debut against Sheffield Wednesday and I wasn't on the losing side for the remainder of that season.

'We were a team that gave everything. We had to because, off the pitch, Chelsea were fighting for their existence.

'A lot of people disliked Bates in those days and I'm sure he still has enemies because he is that kind of bloke. A bit like me, he says what he feels. But the bottom line is that without him there is no Chelsea.

'I remember Bates calling a team meeting before the 1984/85 season. We had been promoted to the First Division and he wanted to tell us about bonuses and sponsored kit for the forthcoming season. We held the meeting out in the middle of the pitch, Bates standing up and us sitting down. It must have been because he didn't want anyone else to hear.

'It was a period of my career that I loved. I will always have a soft spot for the club and it broke my heart when I left. We had won promotion but then John Neal had to quit because of ill health and that was the beginning of the end for me. Neal knew how to handle me but Hollins didn't have a clue. Hollins taking over was the worst thing that could have happened to the club at that stage.

'He thought that Jerry Murphy was the new Mickey Thomas. Hollins didn't like me commuting from Wales. Neal didn't mind because he knew I could do the business, and always did. It was only a matter of time before I left.

'One day Hollins pulled me aside at the training ground and said that the chairman wanted to speak to me. I went and saw Bates and he told me that Leeds, West Brom and Birmingham were interested in buying me. I didn't even know I was for sale, but things had been going on behind my back and when you have that kind of conversation with the chairman you know your time is up.

'Bates told me that West Brom officials were waiting for me in a hotel down the road. That was quick, I thought. Still, I went along to see them. When we met, the chairman of West Brom immediately told me that I was his son's favourite player. That was a good start. I signed for them and played under Johnny Giles. But it broke my heart to leave Chelsea.

'I have always had a great relationship with supporters and the Chelsea fans were brilliant to me. When I went back to Chelsea with West Brom, and then Stoke, they treated me like a hero. Great days, great side, great club. I still get fan mail from Chelsea fans.

'The club owes a lot to Bates; in fact, they owe him everything. All those cutbacks – players not allowed upstairs and no tickets for this and that – have paid off. Old players still don't get complimentary tickets as far as I know. But who was right? He was. Look at them now.'

When Bates looks back at the John Hollins era he pulls no punches. 'It was a complete disaster.'

Hollins had been one of the great Chelsea players. He began in the Osgood and Hudson team and stayed while other stars were sold off and new eras built. He played under Dave Sexton, Ron Suart, Eddie McCreadie, Ken Shellito, Danny Blanchflower, Geoff Hurst and John Neal, when he worked as first-team player-coach.

Neal has made it clear that he did not respect him and Bates now regrets giving him the job. Hollins seems to have split up a successful side too quickly, a side that certainly could have brought the club more success and generated more revenue.

Hollins eventually lost the respect of the players and it led to furious rows between Bates and the playing staff. Hollins was his appointment and he challenged the players to get on and co-operate with the management, or else.

Typical of Bates's attacks on the players during the 1986/87 season was this kind of challenge: 'The other day, one of our players said he had lost his enthusiasm for the game. I have seen no corresponding loss of enthusiasm for picking up his pay cheque. Funny that.

'I told Kerry Dixon that he would get a new contract if he had a good World Cup. He played ten minutes in Mexico and came back admitting that the only thing he had improved was his tennis. But he still wanted a new contract.

'The players who don't get on with John Hollins have to accept that he is my manager. He has the job until he wants to retire. Hollins is intelligent, ambitious and honest – underline that word honest; it is the most important quality of all these days. And we are going to do it his way.

'Players will have to conform to the club and not the other way round. If they won't then they will go at our convenience because I am not looking for money, only a strengthening of the team and we will get new players who will do it our way. It is as simple as that.

'I am interested in recruiting players of character; mature and preferably married players. My players should realise that I know more about their characters than they might imagine.' This again emphasises how much in control Bates was. He had done his homework on all his players; he was running his eye over them and knew about their every move. It is, of course, no surprise then to see why Bates has kept his spies out all the way through. Players he did not respect or want, Matthew Harding and other enemies . . . they were all watched carefully. Bates had a dossier on them all.

Bates, in fact, accused star striker Dixon of starting the troubles of 1986/87. It led to ten players asking for transfers that season. The Chelsea players even called in PFA chief executive Gordon Taylor as a peacemaker. It was the worst bust-up since Peter Osgood, Alan Hudson and the rest fell out with Dave Sexton.

It was just another death wish, it seemed, for a club with a history of building a side and then destroying it. Bates wanted to re-build the club and at this stage Chelsea were back on their feet financially, although still fighting the property developers. The last thing he needed was a brush between manager and players. But he had appointed Hollins and he knew that he had to stick with him.

Dixon had admitted at the start of the season that he and David Speedie had had a punch-up. Bates never forgave Dixon and he said, 'The problems date back to Dixon's remarks two days before the start of the season. It set a bad example before our opening game, talking about punching Speedie.

'That incident happened a few years before but you can imagine what effect it had on his playing relationship with Speedie. It affected the atmosphere in the dressing room and the spirit between players, who started to slag each other off. What is worse, it gave the players who had left the club the chance to join in, and they are still doing it.

'But the barrack-room lawyers are becoming less of an influence as John Hollins begins to build the club and his own image.

'If those players who are moaning really want to go then they can all bugger off to other clubs, then perhaps they will appreciate just how well off they were at Chelsea. The players who have been bellyaching have enjoyed unbroken success for three years. Suddenly they started to lose so they didn't get their win bonuses – so they were unhappy. What did they want then, more wages? But why the hell should they get more for losing?

'Listen, I am well enough off not to take any nonsense. I am my own worst critic. I am a perfectionist but I never make bigger demands on my staff than I can fulfil myself.'

For the first time in his Chelsea career, Bates had to dismiss rumours that he was interfering with Hollins and even selecting the side. 'It's not true,' he said. 'Why don't you ask the manager? If I tried to pick his team, Holly would tell me to get stuffed.

'I do not run the club. I run the business side of the club but the football is down to John Hollins. I have been the only friend he has had during the trouble of this season. It is wrong to say that he is a puppet of mine. I advise only whether or not we can afford to buy a certain player. Managers are not equipped for that side of the business. Those who think they are had better know what they are doing.' These are the exact sentiments that Bates carries with him today.

PFA chief executive Taylor accused Bates of stoking up trouble and demanded he show his players more dignity. Bates's answer was to tell Taylor to mind his own fucking business. Chelsea star, centre half Joe McLaughlin, accused Bates of being ignorant and sarcastic. By now, the Chelsea war was in full cry. The players and their union on one side, Hollins and Bates on the other. There was only one winner, and it wasn't the PFA. It wasn't Hollins either.

Hollins was not the manager Chelsea needed. His appointment was a mistake. He did not have enough personality, he failed to gain the respect of the players and his relationship with the media was a joke. At one stage he drew an imaginary line on the pavement outside the dressing-room area at Stamford Bridge. The journalists were not allowed to cross the line as they waited for interviews after each game. The stewards would guess where the line was and the media made fun of it, jumping across it and asking if this was too close for Hollins. It all became silly, a huge joke, and everyone lost respect for Hollins. Bates included.

Hollins was still in charge of the team for the start of the following season, somehow surviving the pressure from inside the club. But there was only one man in complete control, and that was Ken Bates. He kept an eye on everything that was happening, inside and outside his football club.

He clashed continually with the media. 'I'm off to my 300-acre farm, you lot can bugger off to your council houses,' was his favourite Saturday-night goodbye to them.

Bates introduced closed-circuit television and family enclosures. He claims that in 1987 he had seventeen First Division clubs lined up to withdraw from the FA Cup if a Bates-led campaign did not get its way. What was it over? Now he thinks about it hard and says, 'The quality of the tea?' Who cared? Another day, another battle. He was the first to advocate a national police task force on hooliganism and restrictions on convicted hooligans travelling abroad – years before it happened.

Bates is coarse, but he is refreshing at the same time. People were, and are, scared of him because he says what he feels. 'I am difficult to deal with because I am not logical,' he says. 'I say what people think. What is wrong with that?'

Bates without the mischief would not be Bates. He rarely loses his temper, rarely screams and shouts, but he gets his point across. If he doesn't get his own way, he walks out. Now he recalls, 'I made people think. Those electric fences. No one was going to do anything until I did something. OK, people didn't like it, they don't like me at times, but I like to think I get things done. Don't think about it, do it, that's my motto. Those electric fences stirred people in high places. You could say they got a shock.'

At that stage Bates, it seems, was in complete control of everything except the managerial situation. By early 1988, the players were still struggling to respect John Hollins and the club were lurching towards relegation. At the end of March, Bates decided that Hollins had to go. He had to eat humble pie and part company with someone he had defended and stood by for so long. But Bates is no fool. He knew that Chelsea must not be relegated, and that was a distinct possibility under Hollins.

He regretted having to make the decision and admitted, 'I still think that one day John Hollins will become a great manager. I have regrets and feel sad about what has happened.'

Bates, in the end, sacked Tom Walley, the coach Hollins wanted in but the man the players detested most. Bates knew how the players felt and had been urging Hollins to change his coach in order to bring harmony and respect to the first-team squad. Hollins refused and so Bates acted for the good of the club. He sacked Walley first, hoping that it would satisfy the players. Five weeks later, the end came for Hollins.

Bates said at the time, 'I regret that John didn't listen to advice that the right people were trying to give him. Instead, he chose to listen to the advice offered by others. The whole situation is very sad. It is sad that a manager could not talk to his chairman about football matters. But something had to change. If results are not going right, and they were not, then the chairman and the board have to ask themselves what is happening. Decisions have to be made.'

Bates had brought in Bobby Campbell, the former Arsenal coach and Fulham manager, as coach when he sacked Walley. Campbell was now promoted to caretaker manager. His job was to end the run of eighteen games without victory and keep Chelsea in the First Division. He failed. These were depressing times for Bates and his club.

It is funny how the passing of time alters one's perspective. When Hollins was his manager, Bates defended him vigorously. When Hollins left Chelsea, Bates wished him well and predicted that one day he would make a great manager. Now, however, Bates says of the Hollins era, 'He was disastrous. He simply would not get rid of Tom Walley when everyone told him that Walley was the reason things were going badly. John asked for advice but never took it. I was close to John Neal but never had the same relationship with Hollins. Let's say I was close . . . ish.

'I also don't believe that his wife did him any favours. She pushed him hard, she was ambitious for him. There is a big step up when you go from coach to manager. When you are coach, you not only have a responsibility to the manager, you are also a shoulder to cry on for the players. You are a go-between, a buffer if you like. When you become a manager, you have to change. You can no longer be a friend of the players. You have to be strong and make decisions.'

Bates made another strong decision in the summer of 1987. He made Campbell manager, despite relegation. He appointed from within again, despite the disappointments of the Hollins era.

'We were relegated,' recalls Campbell, 'but we came straight back up as Champions of the Second Division. We got 99 points, scored 96 goals and, without question, we won it in style. It was a mess off the pitch with Ken Bates fighting to keep the club solvent. I have no doubts that had we not gone back up then Chelsea Football Club would have folded. I don't believe that the supporters realised just how serious it was; they saw only our success on the pitch.'

Chelsea only lost five matches all season. Amazingly, three of those setbacks came within the first six games. Chelsea did not win until 24 September, a 2–0 away win at Leeds, but there was no turning back after that. 'We played fantastic football,' said Campbell. 'I signed my players, inherited others, and built a damn good team.

'My first signing was goalkeeper Kevin Hitchcock from Mansfield, who has proved himself a marvellous servant for the club and is still going strong today. Graham Roberts, the former Spurs and Rangers defender, was my captain – Captain

Fantastic. He was a real inspiration to everyone around him and the crowd loved him.

'I signed goalkeeper Dave Beasant from Newcastle; Kerry Dixon was still going strong and Gordon Durie was his partner up front; old jukebox, Johnny Bumstead played the best football of his career; little McAllister was on the wing and then we had will-o'-the white (Kevin Wilson) and will-o'-the-black (Clive Wilson). I also signed two of the first foreign players to play in English football – defenders Ken Monkou from Holland and Erland Johnsen from Norway. Ken is still playing here with Southampton and Erland has only just gone back to his home country.

'I liked to have a bit of style in the team. I had worked with Terry Venables's team at QPR, which included Stan Bowles, and, at Arsenal, I worked closely with one of the best players of all, Liam Brady. There were also people like Frank Stapleton and David O'Leary in that Arsenal side. Then, at Fulham, I witnessed one of the most exciting eras for that club, with George Best, Rodney Marsh and Bobby Moore. So, I always insisted on some stylish, attractive football.'

The signing of Roberts, on 9 August 1988, eventually turned into a nightmare for Bates. The two men became arch enemies after Roberts shopped Bates to the Football League and triggered the countdown to a then record £105,000 fine.

It was alleged that Roberts received a £100,000 payment over the sale of his house in Scotland and that Bates promised him a similar deal on another house. Bates pleaded his innocence but the League still fined Chelsea. Bates said at the time, 'Roberts was a tainted witness. And the only witness.' Chelsea were also found guilty of illegal payments to Gareth Hall and Kerry Dixon. Chelsea and Bates denied the charges, and still do today.

Bates believes that decision by the League was to get back at him, for all the things he had done and said about the running of the game. 'Was the decision pre-judged because of me? That is what I kept asking the commission but they refused to comment. I had ruffled a few feathers and I am sure a lot of people took great delight in what had happened at my club.

Yes, I believe that I was a contributory factor in Chelsea being found guilty.

'But I have always felt that you should fight for what you believe in and fight hard. You have to keep battling because one day you will win.'

Campbell tried to keep all the money fights and the political storms away from the players. He says, 'As manager, all the off-pitch stuff was hard because I realised just how serious it was. But the players are rarely affected by such times. I blocked it out and made sure none of the financial crises filtered through to the squad. Managers come and go but players always survive. They are tough mentally and they perform regardless of what is happening around them.'

Campbell and Bates first became friendly when, as manager of Fulham, Bobby, and his wife Susan, went to watch Chelsea play. In an after-match conversation Susan Campbell said to Pam Bates, 'If you want to watch a good game come and visit Fulham.' A few months later, Campbell's secretary took a message from a Mr Bates and Campbell had no idea who it was. Then he remembered the evening at Chelsea, put two and two together, invited them to Fulham as his guests and a friendship was formed. Bates once said, 'The last person I would give a job to is Bobby Campbell. I would rather keep him as a friend.'

But he did give Campbell a job, as first-team coach under Hollins after Walley had been sacked. Hollins always felt that Campbell had been planted to oust him but both Campbell and Bates deny this. They certainly became friends. Bates is now godfather to Campbell's youngest son, Luke, and, estranged wife Pam is his godmother. The other godfather is comedian Jimmy Tarbuck.

Campbell adds, 'When I was manager no one could have fought harder for the club than Ken Bates. He certainly took on all-comers off the pitch. No doubt there were things he didn't tell me about, and I only have admiration for his determination.

'We won promotion and then, in our first year back in the First Division, we finished fifth.' Three times that season

Chelsea were actually top. 'We were ahead of the rest for about ten days,' remembers Campbell. 'It was another superb effort and had it not been for the European ban on English players we would have taken the club into Europe the following season.' Kerry Dixon was again top scorer, with twenty goals.

Perhaps the biggest coup of Campbell's Chelsea career was attracting Glenn Hoddle to the club. Campbell had built one side and had success. He knew that he needed to re-build, promote youngsters and have a ten-year plan for Chelsea. He had the youngsters like Graeme Le Saux, Craig Burley, Frank Sinclair, Graeme Stuart and Damien Matthew. There was also a twelve-year-old called Michael Duberry who Campbell knew was going to be a star. What he needed was an old head to coax them along. It came to him. Glenn Hoddle was perfect. He rang Hoddle's agent, Dennis Roach, to be told that his timing was uncanny. Monaco were just releasing Hoddle from his contract because of injury. Campbell says, 'Roach told me I must be psychic and I instantly knew that this move was meant to be.

'Chelsea needed something special, the fans deserved something special, and I wanted to go on to something bigger. Hoddle was ideal. We talked and he agreed to come to the club, train, have treatment and see if he could get fit again.'

After five months, Campbell knew the time was right for Hoddle's return to the English game. Campbell remembers, 'I told him that I had handpicked the game for him. I said that the opposition were a footballing side who couldn't knock the skin off a rice pudding. It would certainly not be a kicking match.' Hoddle, however, was not keen. He did not feel confident enough. 'He told me he couldn't do it. Something was holding him back,' said Campbell. 'I assured him that I would take full responsibility.'

Hoddle never played for Chelsea at first-team level. Campbell failed to persuade him. The opposition he had lined up for him, Luton, took on Chelsea without the hidden weapon. Luton, in fact, were leading 3–0 at one stage after Le Saux had been sent off. Chelsea came back to draw 3–3 and

Campbell could only reflect on what might have been. 'For a start, he would have put ten thousand on the gate,' says Campbell. 'It would also have pushed the kids on much quicker than I was able to do. But something held him back.'

Hoddle eventually decided that management, more than the First Division, was for him. Maybe he was too worried about his fitness, or the image he had left behind at Spurs, the image of a world-class player, and he did not want to fall below that standard. He went to Swindon as player-coach. He built a superb footballing side in the West Country, playing as sweeper and taking Swindon into the First Division. But Chelsea's seed had been sown and eventually he was to return, and how.

The end for Campbell came when Bates asked him to move upstairs as general manager. Bates had done the same with Neal and history was repeating itself. 'People still ask me why I left,' says Campbell. 'For three years Ken gave me no grief, no interference. I was often asked about Ken and people told me how he interfered with team affairs. I corrected them because it just was not true.'

Campbell does however believe that certain people inside Stamford Bridge talked to Bates about him and influenced a decision to push him into the boardroom. He knows who they are but has pledged never to name names. He adds, 'Ken said to me, "Come upstairs and help me run the club." I said no and, for a spell, I was left to run the team, but he kept trying to persuade me.'

Campbell's wife was keen for him to become general manager. She argued that he had worked himself to a standstill in football and it was his reward. Reluctantly, under pressure from home and the office, he agreed. It was a decision he was to regret immediately. He soon realised that he was not a boardroom man, he was a players' man who needed to be out with the team on the training pitch.

Ironically, it was Campbell who was in at the start of the planning of Bates's dream. He says, 'I helped organise the plans for the hotel, the car parks, everything. But as I was doing it I thought to myself, I am doing this when I should be doing the football. I was never happy. No, never fulfilled.'

One incident took Campbell over the top in his relationship with Bates, which had become strained since his move upstairs. His wife and son were stopped coming into the club to meet Bobby for a match-day boardroom lunch. Bobby heard about the block and rushed downstairs to confront a member of the Chelsea staff who was demanding to know where Susan had got her boardroom ticket from.

At nine o'clock on Monday morning, Campbell demanded a meeting with Bates and resigned. Bates said that he knew nothing about the incident. Campbell did not believe him and told him where to stick his job. Campbell, in fact, did resign, even if the record books do say that he was sacked. To this day, he has never forgiven the member of staff who blocked his wife and was so rude to her.

Campbell has no regrets. He talks to Bates occasionally and still counts him as a friend. He says, 'I put everything I had into that job. All my experience and more. If I did make a mistake then it was agreeing to go upstairs.

'I helped turn the club around and then . . . There is a lot more I could say but I have never gone public, and never will, with the whole story. I will say one thing. When I was at Chelsea, Ken Bates had three good friends – his wife, Yvonne Todd and me.'

Campbell is left with his memories, and his record. He is proud of the things he achieved, even little incidents like the money he got for Scottish international Pat Nevin at a transfer tribunal. 'Pat didn't want to go but he had become so disillusioned with the previous management (Hollins and Walley) that he decided he would. He said that had I been around for the previous twelve months, he would not have left. But, by the time I arrived, he was involved in talks with Everton and the deal was inevitable. Chelsea had told Pat that he did not figure in their plans, amazing really. Everton had bid £250,000 but I said that I wanted one million. I had been the first manager to go to a tribunal (when Spurs signed John Lacy from Fulham) and so I knew how they operated.

'At the tribunal I was asked where I got my figures from. I said that Pat Nevin was entertainment, he put bums on seats

Left The end of season 1995/96 and Glenn Hoddle bids the fans a fond farewell

Below A year later, Eddie Newton scores the winning goal in the FA Cup final against Middlesbrough

Top right Dennis Wise, Chelsea's influential captain holds aloft the FA Cup

Bottom right Ruud Gullit, Ken Bates and Colin Hutchinson

Above Before

Left After

Top right Ruud Gullit and Gianluca Vialli

Bottom right Ken Bates with David Mellor

Above With Bobby Campbell

Left Vialli's first training session as the new player/manager

Top right Gianfranco Zola scores the only goal to beat Stuttgart in the Cup Winners Cup final in May 1998

Bottom right Wise, Zola and Tore Andre Flo celebrate a mighty achievement

Above Dennis Wise holds the cup aloft while behind him Dan Petrescu, Franck Lebeouf, Steve Clarke, Gianfranco Zola, Danny Granville and Gianluca Vialli celebrate

Left The departing hero, Mark Hughes, Hoddle's first signing, leaves Chelsea for the South Coast, joining Southampton at the start of the 1998/99 season

and generated money for the club. I said that he was in the same bracket as other entertainers I had worked with, including Liam Brady and Alan Ball. I then explained that Liverpool had just paid £900,000 to Watford for John Barnes. The chairman of the meeting smirked. I got £925,000. Chelsea were shocked, but not half as shocked as Everton.'

Bates now likens Campbell to Stan Cullis, the former great manager of Wolves who led them to such glory in the fifties and early sixties. 'He would force people to do things. I thought Bobby would be a good general manager but he didn't want to know. He wanted to be on the pitch all the time with the players. He is still a friend of mine.'

Amazingly, Chelsea and Bates again turned to the coach and promoted from within. This time it was Ian Porterfield, the Scot who had scored Sunderland's FA Cup Final winning goal against Leeds in 1973. He had been Campbell's first-team coach and Bates made the decision to give him the job. It proved to be disastrous.

It is interesting to analyse Bates's appointments. He inherited John Neal and promoted John Hollins. He then appointed from within when Bobby Campbell took over. Porterfield was next, another internal appointment, and then he went outside for David Webb and Glenn Hoddle. Following Hoddle's exit for England he stayed inside Stamford Bridge by promoting Ruud Gullit and then Gianluca Vialli. Even Webb was a former Chelsea hero, and Hoddle was certainly known to the club after his training and treatment sessions there. It means that not once has Bates appointed a stranger in sixteen years. A sure sign of his emphasis on loyalty. He has also lost two of his managers after asking them to move upstairs into the boardroom. 'And I have only sacked two,' he says. 'Hollins and Porterfield. That record doesn't portray a fitting image for those people who call me ruthless and hard.'

In 1991/92 Chelsea finished fourteenth under Porterfield and the following season eleventh. Bates had had enough long before he was sacked. He explains, 'Porterfield was a disaster. He used to make long rambling speeches in his thick Scottish accent that I couldn't understand.

'There were times, especially in his last six months, when I couldn't bear to talk to him. I would say to Colin Hutchinson, "Colin, you take over, I can't stand him." Like Hollins, in the end we had to get rid of him quickly. I believe that he was thinking of resigning himself throughout the six months before we acted. The team were sliding, we had to make a decision.'

Campbell was not surprised and recalls, 'I took Porterfield on and soon realised that he had problems at home. I would let him go home straight after training. It was his job to warm up the players and I would then go out and work with them.

'But we all think we are better than we are and he went around telling people that he did all the training, especially when we were having success. It's called brainwashing. I should have told Batesy that Ian Porterfield was not the right man for the job.'

Bates remembers well the night that Porterfield was eventually sacked. 'I had planned a weekend away with Suzannah and asked her if she wanted to go to Oxford or Paris. She said Oxford and I booked a honeymoon suite in a nice hotel. We were booked in for three days and the first night I spent pacing the floor trying to figure out who to get as manager. "We have sacked Porterfield, so who should come in?" I kept asking. Suzannah was very impressed. What a great break for her that turned out to be.'

There are many people who believed that it was Porterfield who made one of the biggest transfer cockups of all time by selling Graeme Le Saux to Blackburn, for just £600,000 with striker Steve Livingstone going the other way to Stamford Bridge. In fact, it was David Webb who sold Le Saux.

It was an extraordinary giveaway by Chelsea and Porterfield has often carried the can for it. Matthew Harding, for instance, was never happy with the facts of the deal and spent months trying to discover why such a talent was given away so cheaply, an argument that was confirmed when Chelsea bought him back at the start of the 1997/98 season for £4.5 million.

Harding had examined the paperwork and spoken to people about the deal. He did not believe the deal was only £600,000.

He was convinced that something underhand had gone on. It was completely unproven, of course, but it showed his determination to find facts that would bring down Bates.

It was Bates and Colin Hutchinson who eventually decided on David Webb, a member of the side that had won the Cup in 1970. 'Colin told me that Webby was available so I gave him a call and arranged a meeting at the Conrad Hotel for the next day at eleven in the morning. I asked him to keep us in the First Division but made no long-term promises about the job. It was a ninety-day contract, nothing more than that.

'Thank goodness he did it and kept us in the First Division. I will always be grateful to him. He was not sacked because it was never like that. He wasn't too pleased at the time but, again, decisions had to be made. It is interesting that when I asked Webby to do a holding job for me I received a telephone call from his old Southend chairman Vic Jobson, who told me, "You have got a good man, but make him stick to team matters." '

Bates remembered that a comment by Campbell also backs up the notion that Webby always saw himself as more than a coach. 'He fancied himself as a Terry Venables-type figure.' Bates adds, 'Football is like any other business. Football men run the football; financial men run the business. That way, you have a successful company.'

Bates looks back on this period with many memories, huge relief, and his own opinions as to why Chelsea had to wait for so long for big success. 'I believe,' he says, 'that we were hit by three playing tragedies.

'The first was John Neal's heart problems and eventual operation. Had he not had that problem, had he stayed in control, who knows? He might still have been manager today. He knew what he wanted. He knew players misbehaved but he also knew that on the pitch they would do the business for him.

'If there was a weakness, it was the younger players thinking they could also get away with things. I believe that cockiness was the very reason the great Osgood side collapsed. I know that Ossie disagrees. But the 1970 side was made up of star players and second-rate players, and the second-rate players wanted to be Jack the lads too.

'The next generation, after Ossie and Hudson, was not good enough. Micky Droy, Ian Britton, Gary Locke . . . that era . . . they were journeymen. You have to be one hundred per cent dedicated and I am not sure that they were.

'The best team Chelsea have had since Ossie's lot, until now, was the Neal one that had Dixon, Speedie, Jones, Thomas and McLaughlin.'

Tragedy two? 'We never replaced Eddie Niedzwiecki when he was injured. He was one of the great goalkeepers and it was a tragedy when he collapsed under Steve Wicks in a cup replay against QPR. He was seriously injured and we should have moved quickly to sign a replacement. But John Hollins fudged. He couldn't make up his mind and we lost valuable time.

'Then, of course, there was the sickening injury that ended the career of Paul Elliot.

'Those things, I believe, changed the course of those seasons and changed the course of history at the club. I recall having to win at Charlton to avoid relegation. Colin West was going through when he was blatantly elbowed down by Paul Miller, once of Spurs and one of Harding's mates. The referee didn't give a penalty, even though it was as clear as day. Had we won we would have stayed up.

'These things stick in the mind. I can still see West lying face down in the mud when the final whistle blew, with no one going to him. I also recall Jim Lawton writing in the *Express* the next day, "What was the chairman doing looking over the pitch at the final whistle?" I was worried about West, that is what I was doing.'

Perhaps one of the biggest memories of all would be the signing of Glenn Hoddle as manager. Long before he called David Webb into his office to tell him that he was not making him manager, Bates had thought long and hard about a manager for the future.

He knew that his club, and indeed football, had reached a turning point. It was getting big and Bates knew that over the next decade it would become a massive multi-million pound concern. He needed a big name, someone with the ability to take Chelsea on to a different level.

He thought about Glenn Hoddle and the more he thought about him the more he liked the idea. There is no question that Hoddle was tapped up before the season ended, before Hoddle took Swindon to the play-offs and led them into the First Division. Hoddle also liked the idea of the Chelsea challenge. Ambitious himself, he knew that Swindon was only a career stepping stone for him. Chelsea would be ideal. The kind of platform he needed at this stage of his career.

Bates and Hoddle met and Bates outlined his dream to Hoddle. It was the dream that had been in his mind since that day in 1982 when he first walked into the club. Now, in the summer of 1993, eleven years later, he knew that Hoddle was right for the biggest step of all. It was time Chelsea reached up and touched the stars.

Bates now admits that signing Hoddle was one of the most important decisions he made. The sleeping giant awoke. Chelsea were big again. They won things. Hoddle, no doubt, helped Bates towards his dream. It was a good partnership, while it lasted.

Incredibly, Hoddle may not have been given the job if Webb had not sold Le Saux so cheaply. Bates admits that the deal confused and annoyed him. 'I was away on a cruise in Brazil when it happened,' he recalls. 'I returned to discover that we had sold a great player cheaply and bought someone I had not really heard of in return. I understand that Webby had not even seen Livingstone play when he signed him in part-exchange. It was a strange transfer and one that worried me.

'That deal was definitely a factor when we made the change. Just think, had we stayed with Webb, then Hoddle, all this, may never have happened. Getting rid of Webby and bringing in Hoddle was a huge on-pitch turning point for this club. It was the best £5 million we have ever wasted.'

8 The Managers: Glenn Hoddle to Gianluca Vialli

THE ARRIVAL OF GLENN HODDLE got the exact reaction Ken Bates had hoped for. Football stood up and watched with interest, the fans became excited overnight and star players from all over the world noted Hoddle's arrival. In a nutshell, Chelsea, after flirting with success for so long, were now taken seriously. It was a vital moment in the club's history and one of the most significant moments of Ken Bates's career in charge – a breakthrough.

Hoddle meant top quality. Hoddle meant success. John Neal, John Hollins, Bobby Campbell, Ian Porterfield and David Webb are all very well, but Glenn Hoddle was something else.

It was a coup for Bates, who had himself reached a crossroads. He knew, deep down, that he was going to win his battle off the pitch so he now needed someone to spearhead an on-pitch challenge.

Hoddle fitted the bill. At that stage, the two men needed each other. The respect didn't last, but it was fun while it did. And so began a significant chapter in Chelsea's history.

In Hoddle's first season, Chelsea reached the FA Cup Final before being beaten 4–0 by Manchester United. If United were to be the yardstick then Chelsea discovered they were still a long way behind the best in England. Bates and his directors noted that with interest. Getting to Wembley was one thing, but they wanted to be winners. They finished fourteenth in the Premiership, not particularly impressive but Bates was happy enough with the development, particularly off the pitch where Hoddle brought a new, professional approach to training, preparation and the facilities at the training ground.

Another good cup run followed the next season, this time in the European Cup Winners' Cup, when they reached the semi-final. Again, they were disappointing in the Premiership, not fulfilling the potential of the squad. There was not enough consistency.

The arrival of Mark Hughes and Ruud Gullit further galvanised Chelsea. Gullit was a really big name, and getting Hughes from Manchester United was another milestone. Here was a forward respected by so many, and a man who had achieved great success. But once more it was in the Cup that Chelsea proved to be successful, reaching the semi-final before going down 2–1 to their old rivals United after Gullit had put them ahead. They were to finish fourteenth yet again in the Premiership.

Hoddle had begun his career as a player in the sweeper role, a position that he enjoyed and one which he encouraged all his sides to play. He signed Gullit to play in the same position, although this led to some conflict among the players, who felt that Gullit was not disciplined enough as a defender to be effective in the Premiership. An injury to Gullit let in David Lee, who produced the best form of his career in Hoddle's spare defender role. Gullit returned to play in midfield, a position that proved to be far more beneficial to the rest of the team.

In the boardroom, Bates and his directors respected Hoddle, for what he had achieved in the game and for what he had brought to Chelsea in such a short time. They will always be grateful to the man who forged the change from mediocrity to expectancy, the change from also-rans to winners.

Something, however, began to nag at Bates. Soon into Hoddle's reign, Bates's war with Harding was at its peak and Bates suspected that Harding and Hoddle were forming a dangerous relationship – dangerous for him, that is. He put out his spies and discovered things that he did not like. Harding, it would appear, was using Hoddle to get closer to what he wanted – the chairmanship and control of Chelsea Football Club. It got so bad that, in the end, Bates did not trust either man.

He hated Harding and grew to distrust Hoddle. It is not a healthy thing, when the chairman dislikes a fellow director and is not so sure about the man in charge of the team. Bates worried about it a lot and spoke about it to those close to him – but he still didn't quite know how to deal with the situation. He fought, of course, banning Harding from the directors' box and making sure that never, and I mean never, would he gain control.

As Bates compiled his dossier on Harding and Hoddle, he was helped by many people, from both inside and outside the club. Bates is no fool. He is an astute man with a razor-sharp mind. He prided himself on knowing everything that was going on behind his back.

Bates looks back at the Hoddle era with mixed feelings. He says, 'I learnt no more about Glenn Hoddle from the day he walked through the door to the day he left.

'He was a listener, not a giver. He did not open up and I respect that. Did we become close? That is a difficult question to answer. Let's just say that we worked together as chairman and manager.

'It was Bobby Campbell who brought Glenn to the club. He allowed him to train, have treatment and stay with us. I think Glenn had one reserve game before Swindon offered him a job. I asked him to return as our manager because I wanted someone to build a platform.

'We had come a long way, on and off the pitch, since I took control, and we had to enter the next stage. David Webb was not the man for that next jump. He was a lovable rogue but I had made up my mind that it would not be Webby, even before the end of that season when he kept us in the First Division.

'Hoddle fitted the bill. I knew he was ambitious, and he had the bonus of knowing the Chelsea players. When he had been here training and getting fit he had been a keen observer. It's funny looking back, but when I first sat down with him I didn't think he was going to be a great manager. I never thought he would go all the way through with us.

'Glenn Hoddle knows exactly what he wants. I would say he was single minded to the point of weakness. When it came to the crunch, I knew that he wouldn't stay with Chelsea.

'I knew that he would do to Chelsea what he did to Swindon – use us as a stepping stone. A stepping stone to his goal, and that was to become the England coach.

'He once said to me that he would never take the England job because it would mean too much pressure on his wife and children. In fact, I thought then that he would go abroad again and manage.

'Before my own eyes I saw Hoddle become too friendly with Harding. There is no question that Matthew used Hoddle as a weapon against me.

'I think Glenn saw Harding as a bottomless pit of money, an avenue for him to get the players he wanted. He was taken in by Harding's lies. Harding kept banging on about Matthew Le Tissier, who was one of Hoddle's favourite players (it is amazing that he has not selected him more for England), and the Le Tissier thing came to a head at one board meeting.

'Harding was there with Glenn, and so was Colin Hutchinson, Mark Taylor and Yvonne Todd. Hoddle said that he could get Le Tissier with Harding's money. (It was at this stage that Hoddle was also trying to sign Paul Gascoigne.) I said I was sick of this thing about Le Tissier but I would go along with it. I challenged Harding to explain how he would finance the deal.

'I said, "OK, let's buy him tomorrow." But the £10 million fee, the £15,000 a week wages, plus the national health insurance, plus the interest, would amount to a £15 million investment. I explained that we would be paying £1.8 million a year for one player and that it would take the amount gained from four of nineteen home games to finance it.

'I then turned to Matthew and asked him about the interest on this £10 million fee. "How do we pay it back and over what period?" I asked him.

'Hoddle looked at me and said that there would not be any interest to pay. I laughed in his face. I turned back to Harding, who looked at Hoddle and said, "There is no such thing as a free lunch."

'The scales fell from Hoddle's eyes. He had been conned. He had been lied to. Harding had told Hoddle that he would finance the Le Tissier deal and Hoddle had believed that it wouldn't have cost the club a penny. It was not the first time that Harding had conned Hoddle, nor the last. He had conned me for years.

'At that stage we were paying him £1.5 million a year rent, plus his loan to buy players carried one per cent interest over the base rate. We were getting nothing from Harding. No one has believed me, but it is a fact. He gained money out of us.

'I once tackled Hoddle over his relationship with Harding. Was he plotting? Was he siding against me? He said no, and I had to believe him.

'I had to trust him. At the start I did. I went to barbecues at his agent Dennis Roach's house and I grew to trust him. He had a dry sense of humour. He was my manager – there had to be a relationship.

'But, eventually, I knew what was going on behind my back. I found out about the real thing with Glenn Hoddle. Why did he not once come to me and ask about what was happening at boardroom level, or with Harding? He never did. I presumed that he was getting all the information he needed, or wanted to hear, from Harding.'

Director Mark Taylor remembers the Le Tissier board meeting well. He says, 'When Ken confronted Matthew over the interest I remember Glenn turning to Matthew and asking him, "Is that right?" When Matthew gave his famous "There is no such thing as a free lunch" reaction, Glenn was stunned.'

Bates was also aware of what was going on inside the Football Association long before they offered Hoddle the England manager's job. 'When we asked Glenn about a new contract he kept finding a reason to put off the talks. Eventually he got his agent to take me to breakfast at the Conrad Hotel and Roach told me what the FA were offering. When they eventually rang to talk to me about Hoddle I was having lunch and Colin Hutchinson took the call. I suppose, in a way, we had done the same to Swindon. Glenn mentioned that to me but I just said that he should have told me when he told them. He should have come clean. But I wished him luck.

'I have no doubts that he is a better international manager than he is a club manager. He can pick who he likes and he can dump them when he likes, with no contractual obligations.

'When you look back at his transfer record it was not that clever. David Rocastle, Paul Furlong, Terry Phelan (although we got out of jail on him), Mark Stein, Scott Minto, Anthony Barness . . . there are some more.

'But I give him credit for changing people's attitudes. Players' attitudes especially. He didn't take shit from anyone, and we respected him for that. I remember the time he got Craig Burley by the scruff of his neck and threw him down the tunnel after Burley had shown dissent after being substituted.

'There is no question that he brought a new, professional approach to Chelsea. He brought in a dietitian, a masseur, a faith healer and other new wave ideas. I thought the dietitian was a waste of time because as soon as backs were turned the players returned to eating hamburgers.

'But by the time Glenn had left, we had a new respect and a new wave of player was attracted to the club. The Hughes transfer, by the way, was all down to Roach, the agent of Hughes and Hoddle. He rang Glenn and told him that he could get Hughes if Chelsea wanted him. That was not a master poach by Hoddle.'

Hoddle has never gone public on his time at Chelsea, other than to say that he would not have left Stamford Bridge had it not been for the England job. Do we believe him? And what would have happened to his relationship with Bates had Hoddle been left stranded inside Stamford Bridge by the death of Harding? We may never know. Hoddle may just tell all in his own autobiography, planned for when his England career ends. Somehow I doubt it.

Chelsea got the answer as to who should replace Hoddle during his last game in control, the final match of the 1995/96 season, a home defeat by Blackburn. Hoddle, ironically, had begun with a home defeat by the same opposition. Throughout the last game the Chelsea fans screamed for Ruud Gullit, the Dutch master who they had taken to their hearts. They wanted Gullit as their player-coach. By the following Friday, Chelsea had persuaded Ruud to take control.

It was a master stroke. If Chelsea wanted to build on the platform laid by Hoddle, here was a man to do it. A superstar of world renown, he began to attract the kind of players Chelsea had only dreamed of. Before Gullit accepted the position of player-manager he asked the Chelsea board if they could match his ambition. Indeed, did they have the financial clout to back his own ideas?

They said yes, and into Chelsea came players like Gianluca Vialli, Gianfranco Zola, Frank LeBoeuf and Roberto Di Matteo. All, as well as Gullit, on £1 million-plus a year contracts.

The 1996/97 season was a fairy tale for Chelsea. And Bates. The stadium was going up rapidly around him and the signs of the dream were growing every time he took his seat in the front row of the directors' box. If I visited Ken for lunch, or just a chat, the girls on the switchboard would laugh and say that I would be back shortly to get my hard hat. 'No,' I would say, 'I have seen around the project already.' But it was no good – Bates was so proud of his dream that any visitor was whisked away on a flying visit, up crane lifts, across muddy puddles, through the restaurants, into the hotel and up to his penthouse. He would stop to hold short conversations with site managers, or the man putting a carpet down. And he knew exactly what was going on. 'This is my living room,' he would say as you stood surrounded by rubble. 'This is the master bedroom and come and take a look at this view over London.' He had every right to be proud, it was magnificent.

On the pitch, Gullit's influence was immense. The fans, other players, indeed the directors, held him in great esteem. In fact, there was hero worship. Hoddle had begun the change, Gullit was taking it on further.

The football that Chelsea played was both entertaining and impressive. They were never out of the top ten and finished sixth. It was the Cup run that caught the imagination once again and so delighted Bates. They had threatened to win something under Hoddle, getting to a final and two semis, but this time they went one further. It was important for the club to win something, to prove to themselves and their supporters that they could be winners again.

Bates agrees. 'The supporters needed it more than anyone. We finally laid the ghost of the seventies. Everyone, including the players had become sick of being compared to the Osgood and Hudson era. Even Steve Clarke, a great Chelsea stalwart, went on record as saying that he was fed up to the back teeth of being told how good Osgood was.

'I believe that since 1982, when I took over, we have improved the team, bit by bit. And there is no point in having a team if you do not have a suitable theatre to play in. I wanted both, and now we have got both. It is not over yet but no one can say that Chelsea and their ground are not top billing.

'In the last four years we have spent a fortune, and we have been able to do that because in that time football, and Chelsea, has gone woooosh!'

Gullit was more of a public figure than Hoddle. A world superstar who had class and a lifestyle that saw him live in a magnificent apartment in London. He had a stunning girlfriend in Estelle Cruyff, the niece of another great Dutch footballer, Johann Cruyff, and he liked to be seen in all the right places around London. The more success he had, the more the sponsors and PR men wanted him. There were clothing and food contracts for him until he was earning just as much outside of football, as he was with Chelsea, and that was a lot.

Gullit had his own style of doing things. He told the players immediately that there would be a squad system, that no one would be a regular. Some did not like it – refused to accept it – and some were sold. John Spencer and Gavin Peacock to QPR for instance. Dennis Wise nicknamed him big nose. Gullit didn't like that but swallowed it because he knew how vital Wise was to a successful Chelsea team.

He also delegated. No reserve matches for him, no scouting, no youth team spying, no administration, no nothing apart from first-team coaching, playing and selecting the team. They were the Gullit rules. They were expensive rules but it usually guaranteed success. Chelsea went along with it, for a time.

They were certainly delighted with the FA Cup Final victory in May 1997, a 2–0 win over Middlesbrough. Di Matteo scored in the opening seconds and the party never stopped.

Eddie Newton, a loyal servant to the club, clinched it in the closing minutes. Bates was overcome with emotion. He hugged Gullit warmly as the Chelsea players filed along the Royal Box, clutching their medals and holding aloft the trophy. Indeed, Gullit almost forgot to join his team, so emotionally involved was he with the occasion. Long after the final whistle, Bates was still in the Royal Box, singing along with the fans and punching the air with pride. It was a magical moment for him, one that he had waited years for.

Who would have thought that a few months later his relationship with Gullit would sour to such an extent that they would part company.

One or two things had already started to nag the Chelsea directors. They were not big things, just those little somethings that you put away to the back of your mind. You know the things, when you say, 'Oh yes, I remember that,' after things have gone wrong. For instance, it was noted that Gullit wore smart clothes and expensive shoes underneath an overcoat while standing on the touchline for one home morning kickoff. They wondered if he was putting a lunch appointment before coaching. There was a comment at director level after the game to the effect that the football had got in the way of the manager's social arrangements.

They also worried about the way he treated Gianluca Vialli, the world star Gullit had signed from Juventus at the start of the season. Vialli was immensely popular with the fans and continued to be the club's top scorer. But there was something wrong between manager and player, the chemistry was not right, and Gullit continually overlooked Vialli, keeping him on the bench even in times of trouble.

It came to a climax in the FA Cup Final against Middlesbrough when Gullit again kept Vialli on the bench until two minutes from the end. Vialli felt humiliated and the directors agreed with him. When Vialli went on for the last two minutes he almost scored and waved goodbye at the final whistle. 'I thought it was my last appearance for Chelsea,' he admitted. 'It was a shame because I love the club.'

These were only small blotches on a superb season for

Chelsea. No one will forget the way they came from 2–0 down to beat Liverpool at home in the FA Cup. But who scored two goals that day? Vialli. There was a growing suspicion inside the club that the manager was jealous of the star attraction.

One or two people also wondered whether Gullit was taking on too much commercially. Was it getting in the way of his day-to-day running of the team?

Bates and Gullit had a good relationship. It grew out of mutual respect and Gullit is on record as saying, 'The chairman leaves me to manage the football team and no one can ask for more than that. I have discovered a lot about this club and I know that there would be no Chelsea without Ken Bates. I am happy to work with him.'

Soon after Gullit was appointed, the two men had lunch and both had a drop too much wine. They laughed, slapped each other on the shoulders and enjoyed the company. It was a bonding session.

But what Gullit eventually found out was that the chairman, the same Bates who drank with him, always has to have respect for his staff. If he loses that then you are dead. And it does not matter if you are one of the biggest names in football. There is always another one.

It started to go wrong for Gullit as Christmas 1997 approached. Chelsea were playing well. They had started a run in the European Cup Winners' Cup and were progressing in the Coca-Cola Cup, despite Gullit putting out weakened sides. They also had one eye on the Premiership. Bates and his Chelsea directors were happy enough. At one board meeting they started to look long term, past the season and into the next one, and even beyond that.

The Chelsea Village scheme was nearing completion and they wondered what the manager had in mind, despite the current season having more than half to run. They also knew that Gullit's contract, signed when he arrived as a player, would soon be up for renewal. It was agreed that Colin Hutchinson would find the right time to ask Gullit about a new contract, and get his thoughts on Chelsea's future. The next step up.

Hutchinson found the time to ask. But he got no positive

answers. So he asked again. Once more, Gullit was not ready to discuss his future. Hutchinson smelt a rat. Why would Gullit, moving towards Cup and League success and being paid a fortune, not want to discuss a new deal? Any other manager in Europe would have jumped at this job.

Hutchinson left it a few more weeks and asked again. Still no response. As the weeks slipped away, the more concerned he became. He reported to the board that there had been no progress but added that, because of team matters and Gullit's other commitments, the manager was struggling to find the time to sit down with Hutchinson. Secretly, Hutchinson told Bates that he was not entirely happy with what was going on. Bates, alerted, started to make his own investigations.

He found out a little more. The dressing room was not as united as the board believed. More than one player was unhappy with the rotating system of selection that Gullit used. A number of others wanted Vialli in the side, but Gullit continued to pick him for just the odd match. He used him more in Europe and in Cup games than in the League.

Gullit was a millionaire when he arrived at Chelsea. He had been one of the world's great players and Chelsea signed him on a £1 million-plus contract. It was mega money, with Chelsea able to pay out such salaries because of Sky Television's huge investment in the Premiership and various club-based sponsorship deals.

Gullit's contract was for playing only and that did not alter when he was moved up to manager. The Dutchman liked money but had never forced any demands on the club. Indeed, when he first joined, he left two cheques untouched on Colin Hutchinson's desk for two months. The amount was for more than £500,000! He had forgotten about the money until Hutchinson reminded him.

Chelsea's dilemma as they tried to get Gullit to sign a new contract was whether to offer him another playing contract, which would have meant a player-coach agreement, or just the position of manager. The latter is not so lucrative – most players have to take a cut once they become managers. It is a fact of football life. The players are the big earners.

Gullit wanted to play, even though he was rationing his own appearances. The board were not so sure and they finally made up their minds that it was to be a manager-only deal after watching Gullit play at centre half in the first leg of the Coca-Cola Cup against Arsenal at Highbury. Gullit, in defence, looked slow and ponderous and was responsible for Arsenal's first goal. Clearly, he was not fit enough.

The management role was offered at £1 million a year, but the board insisted on a swift decision because time was running out for their forward planning. Under the Bosman ruling players were becoming available all over Europe and Chelsea needed a manager in place in order to make their moves and further develop the team.

The irony is that had Gullit said yes and sat down with Hutchinson when Chelsea first asked him to, around October 1997, Gullit would almost certainly be manager today. Why did he delay? Had there been another job lined up for him then he surely would have jumped straight into it when the crunch came with Chelsea.

Was he so arrogant that he thought Chelsea would wait? He had not taken into consideration Ken Bates. When Bates is riled, and he had become frustrated and annoyed at the Gullit delay, it usually ends in tears for the opponent. This time was no exception.

Chelsea called Gullit's bluff. Hutchinson and he eventually did sit down and Gullit said that he wanted to be paid net, with Chelsea picking up the tax. This was the last straw for Bates. His reaction to Hutchinson was, 'Stuff him.'

It is interesting that, when questioned, Bates at first refused to discuss Gullit's future. He was happy to praise him but not able to commit himself about a new contract. 'I have nothing to say on the matter,' he repeated three times when I pressed him.

The Gullit situation nagged away at the media. Stories appeared suggesting that Gullit would go – or that he would stay – and Gullit himself was quoted more than once insisting that there was no problem and that he would be the Chelsea manager next season.

The Chelsea board were so disturbed that they met to discuss a successor. Hutchinson again reported that Gullit had not signed, or indeed committed himself, and the board drew up a short list of five names, four of them foreign and one British. Gianluca Vialli was on the list without him knowing.

It led to an amusing conversation between Vialli and Hutchinson as they boarded the team bus for the next game. The *Sun* had broken the story about Chelsea's short list and Vialli said to Hutchinson as they moved towards the bus steps, 'Why am I not on the list?' 'How do you know you are not?' was the reply.

The longer Gullit delayed, the more the speculation rose. It had to come to a crunch, and it did. Chelsea would not pay net and Hutchinson was sent for one last meeting with Gullit, this time at the club's training ground at Harlington, close to Heathrow Airport. Hutchinson explained to him the board's thoughts and Gullit was not happy. He walked out in the middle of their conversation. Hutchinson waited at the training ground for some time before he was informed that Gullit had indeed driven off. It could only happen in football. The players training, the manager gone and the chief executive waiting to finish his conversation, sitting alone in an office.

It was Gullit's last gesture as Chelsea manager. It was the most controversial exit of any manager under Bates's rule. Gullit was popular and successful and there were many who thought that he was the man to lead the club to the Championship.

In his press conference, the next day, Gullit looked stunned. He demanded to know the real reason why he had been dismissed. 'There must be a real reason,' he said. 'I want to know why I have been kicked out.'

Hutchinson and other Chelsea officials watched with interest as Gullit, live on television, looked into the camera and asked for reasons. Within hours the club had gone public, condemning Gullit for being too greedy and for letting his responsibilities slip.

Let Bates and Colin Hutchinson tell the story in more detail. Bates says, 'Ruud protested that he didn't know the real reasons. Had he not walked out of a meeting with Colin Hutchinson, with Colin in mid sentence, then he would have found out. But Ruud has a reputation for walking out.

'To avoid any possible misunderstanding, here are the facts from Chelsea. The reasons why Ruud Gullit left.

'He wanted to sign a two-year player-coach contract sometime later in the season. We wanted him to sign a three-year coaching-only contract and that was first offered to him last October.

'We could not afford to be caught out again. We were left high and dry by Glenn Hoddle when he kept prevaricating.

'We were unwilling to allow Ruud to continue playing because to play regularly you have to be really fit and train regularly. Ruud was not prepared to do that because he took on so many other outside commitments.

'Chelsea could hardly ask the other players to toe the line if he didn't. He was the manager, after all. An interesting point is that in eighty-four competitive matches since he took over as coach he started just ten and came on as a sub in fourteen of the others. Any club in the land would dispense with a player with such a non-appearance record.

'Ruud said, rightly, that it is up to him to decide when to play or not, or indeed when to finish playing. That's OK. On the other hand, it is the club's right to decide if they want him to continue playing and what price they are prepared to pay.

'We did want Ruud to stay as coach and were even willing to pay him more than Alex Ferguson, who is the most successful manager in England.

'When we did get down to talking money and he made it clear that he wanted a package that would cost us £3.7 million, plus bonuses, we knew it was the end of the road.

'And that is the story. It was an irreconcilable difference of opinion on roles and values.

'There was certainly no clash of egos, as was written and claimed, between Gullit and Bates. In all the time Ruud was at Chelsea we never had a cross word. We didn't see much of each other but when we did meet he made me laugh. I liked his company. I was delighted with all his personal publicity because it helped promote Chelsea and made us one of the highest profile clubs around. Not once did I resent his outside work, which was good for the club and the Village.

'The last words he said to me were, "Please give my love to Suzannah. We must stay friends because this world is a very small one." I hope we do stay friends because I have nothing against Gullit, other than he asked for too much money.

'We had to make a simple decision. Did we want a player-coach at £3.7 million a year or the opportunity, post-Bosman, to acquire another two or three world-class players. Colin Hutchinson, who runs the football side of things, chose the latter.

'Chelsea Football Club is a subsidiary of Chelsea Village and, like all subsidiaries, it is expected to balance its books. Each year we prepare a budget, first estimating our income. From that we deduct all non-playing expenses and what is left is the playing budget that is ring fenced. Colin Hutchinson is the club's managing director and has unfettered control of that sum of money. Provided he keeps within his budget, he has autonomy. Any proceeds of player sales is added to his budget, but if he wants to exceed it then he makes his case to the Chelsea Village board because, at the end of the day, they will have to find the cash.

'Colin, of course, discusses matters with me as he did with Gullit. The Gullit decision was one he discussed with me for some time because of its huge implications. It came down in the end to the fact that he could not afford to give so much of his budget to one man. In addition, the commitment being offered in return was being prejudiced by Ruud's ever-increasing personal activities.

'I can also discount any pressure put on us by the City. It was based on good housekeeping. We could not afford Ruud Gullit. You have to balance your books and keep within your budget, no matter who you are.'

When the decision finally came, Chelsea acted so quickly that part of the board meeting was held by fax. Decisions were taken and explained among men sitting in separate offices right across London. Chelsea had also interviewed and appointed

Vialli before they announced that Gullit had been sacked. It was perhaps the biggest decision made under Bates's rule.

Bates says that Gullit's outside activities did not bother him, but the time he spent away from the club did, if that makes sense. There was certainly a feeling that Gullit's lifestyle had an adverse effect on his control of situations. Bates added, 'If Gullit wants the harsh reality then we were not prepared to pay so much for a part-time playboy manager who carried out his lucrative commercial contracts at the expense of training. Ruud keeps pushing for answers but we cannot make it much clearer. We could not afford him and also he, in our opinion, was putting one or two personal things before us.

'I think it is sad that in the end Ruud demeaned himself. We have since found out that he was delaying on a contract because of personal problems that had nothing to do with Chelsea.

'In the end, Chelsea's interest had to come first. We cannot keep on explaining this.'

In his autobiography, released after the sacking, Gullit does not go into enough detail to satisfy his side of the row. He constantly said that he did not know the real reasons and then failed to answer Chelsea's claim of greed, personal problems and delaying tactics. There were rumours of problems with his financial commitment to his wives and children. Gullit never opened up about those and he left asking questions but never really answering any.

He said that Hutchinson knifed him in the back over the contract. Again, that was unfair and Hutchinson, the man at the very heart of the situation, was forced to respond. He certainly would not have got involved had Gullit not said at his own press conference that he had asked for £2 million. 'That is all,' he said looking straight at the camera lens.

Hutchinson listened to Gullit and decided that the Chelsea fans needed to know the truth. He explains, 'I wanted to keep Ruud Gullit, the club did and so did the fans. We were all gobsmacked at having to part company.

'I came to Chelsea in 1987. Before I took my seat on the board the club had taken some terrible stick for standing by a manager for too long, staying faithful to a man who was having difficulties. The board decided on that occasion that there was not to be a knee-jerk reaction. It was an honourable decision.

'Looking back, John Hollins was relieved of his duties too late. Bobby Campbell couldn't prevent the club being relegated. We learnt from this experience, as was demonstrated five years later. Despite a good start to the 1992/93 season, from early December we went twelve games without a win and appeared to lose our way. We decided to relieve Ian Porterfield of his duties. Maybe he would have done better, maybe he would have sorted it out. We had to make a decision.

'Unlike in the Hollins situation, we acted quickly.

'We brought in David Webb and he did well. But we knew that we were reaching a stage at Chelsea when we had to put down some long-term plans. We wanted entertaining football for the supporters and we needed someone to take us into a new era.

'We appointed Glenn Hoddle. I think almost everyone connected with football, certainly Chelsea, will admit that we got that one right.

'But with the parting of Glenn we learned new lessons. We tried desperately hard to pin him down to a new contract and he stalled. In the end he told us in the last week of the season that he would be leaving. It left us in what could have been a very difficult position.

'However, we had a great alternative on our own doorstep. We asked Ruud to take over and didn't think it was a gamble. We knew he had no managerial experience but by appointing quickly we were able to complete the summer signings of Vialli, Di Matteo and Frank LeBoeuf.

'This is vital in today's transfer market. Players become available and you have to act quickly. And you have to have a positive manager to direct and lead you to where he wants to go.

'But Hoddle's late decision was a lesson, and there is no way we could be caught in that position again.

'I had tried to pin Ruud down since October but he had delayed and delayed. I finally got him down to a date for talks,

Thursday 5 February, but he was still wanting to delay it another month.

'As a club we couldn't wait any longer. It isn't just the Hoddle situation returning to haunt us, it is the Bosman transfer ruling too. You can now talk to a player who is going to be out of contract six months in advance. You can make a pre-contract contract with a player, binding him when his current agreement runs out. Most European footballers end their contracts on 30 June, and that meant any player out of contract was approachable on 1 January.

'It makes life impossible if you do not have the commitment of your own manager. And how can an incoming player feel comfortable when he doesn't know if the manager is staying? Who is he signing for?

'I had to tell Ruud that we had to get on with it. I told him that a decision had to be made, for the club's and the fans' sake.

'At that meeting on 5 February, the talks were amicable. He told me the players he would like to sign for the new season. Then we turned to his contract. He said he was looking for two years. It was then that I told him that the board wanted him to concentrate on coaching and that we were not prepared to keep on paying him as a player.'

It was at that point, I believe, that Gullit knew that his future was away from Chelsea. Unless the club changed their mind. He was never going to sign a manager-only contract. He admitted many times, 'I want to play, I still love to play. I want to carry on as long as my legs allow.' It was the stumbling block, perhaps even more than the money. Gullit had been a world superstar as a player. His pride told him that he could still compete with the best around Europe. It was sad, a man refusing to accept that he had come to the end of a glittering playing career.

Hutchinson adds, 'Ruud made it clear that he was not going to be dictated to. He said that he would know when Ruud Gullit was to hang up his boots.

'I was not dictating that he gave up. The board was quite happy for him to continue being registered as a player and to use himself when he thought fit, but we were not able to continue with his current situation.

'In his first season as a player he was breathtaking, and a structure was put in place whereby he could continue playing. Graham Rix, Gwyn Williams and myself took care of various "old" management chores, thus allowing him to play. We wanted him to.

'But in over eighteen months he started only ten games, which made it clear that playing was not a priority for him. What is more, he had allowed his level of fitness to fall below that which is required of a player in the Premiership.'

This is interesting. Gullit said he wanted to play. Chelsea say that he was not worth his place in the team.

Hutchinson also revealed that Gullit had a clause in his contract that, if he stopped playing, would allow him to continue as a manager only, but at a vastly reduced salary. Why then did Gullit allow his fitness to deteriorate? He knew he was cutting his own throat.

The new contract that Chelsea offered Gullit did not represent such a drop, but there was a cut. Hutchinson explains, 'All top players take cuts when they finish. Why should a club pay huge amounts of money to someone who is no longer playing?

'You would not believe the drop Graham Rix took when he stopped playing to become youth team manager. But he knew that it was a step on the managerial ladder for him.

'Ruud should have realised that we were offering him the chance to start his managerial career, with no apprenticeship and without a coaching badge – something that he could not have done in Italy or Holland.

'Listen, Ruud Gullit was fantastic for Chelsea. We loved every minute of him, but we had to move on. Towards the end we were never quite sure where he was or what he was doing. One day he rang to ask Gwyn Williams to take training, because he was going to be late. He was in Amsterdam.

'Ruud was offered £1 million a year. That would have made him the highest paid manager in English football.'

Chelsea knew that the average salary for a Premiership manager was around £350,000–£400,000. One or two, like

Alex Ferguson and Kenny Dalglish, are paid more, but no one would have been near Gullit. Again, he must have known that. He must also have realised that success would have brought him rich rewards, and even another job back home in Holland or in Italy where he will always be idolised.

Chelsea were staggered when Gullit demanded £2 million net. That would have been £3,320,000 gross. Gullit would also be receiving bonuses, company car and a luxury home. In all, Chelsea would have been paying Gullit around £4 million a year.

'I just could not sanction it,' adds Hutchinson. 'The bottom line is that Ruud became too expensive for us.

'It would have meant us not being able to go into the transfer market for world-class players. It wouldn't have been in the best interest of the team, or the long-term interest of the club.

'Chelsea would have set a precedent had we agreed. It would have been dangerous.

'I believe it was unreasonable for Ruud to expect to be paid three times as much as Alex Ferguson at Manchester United.

'I told him frankly that his demands were ridiculous and that if he was going to continue along the same lines then we would have to find another manager.'

The meeting ended, although a few days later Gullit contacted Hutchinson. He wanted to discuss new players coming in. Hutchinson was surprised after the way the previous meeting had ended. He told Gullit that he would have to come up with different figures if he was to stay as manager.

This is when Hutchinson and Bates got their heads together in the best interests of the club. Hutchinson told Bates that Gullit would not back down. Bates said that Gullit had to go. He agreed one hundred per cent that Gullit was not worth the money.

Gullit would still be manager today had he not been so greedy. It was not as though he was being paid net on his existing contract. It was something new to Chelsea and the demand was way out of reach for them. No manager in English football is paid net. Gullit was paid handsomely, well over £1 million a year and the net figure he took home each month was huge. He wanted more. He thought he could get more. Then he ran into Bates and no one, and I mean no one, is bigger than Bates.

The new man that Bates and Hutchinson had come up with was Gianluca Vialli, their own Italian superstar. Vialli had signed from Juventus at the start of the previous season.

On Monday 9 February, Hutchinson contacted Vialli. Gullit was still the manager at this stage but Chelsea realised that there was now no turning back. The two men spent four hours together. Vialli was stunned at the searching questions posed by Hutchinson, but was sworn to secrecy.

Hutchinson spent the next 48 hours researching Vialli, via a series of telephone calls to Italy. He spoke to about twenty people, checking out Vialli's potential, character and contacts. Hutchinson believed that he had got his man and he and Vialli locked themselves away in Hutchinson's office for four hours on the night of Wednesday 11 February. As England lost 2–0 to Chile under the leadership of a former Chelsea manager, Hutchinson and Vialli shook hands on a deal.

The next day, Hutchinson travelled to the club's training ground to break the news to Gullit. He got no further than to say that his contract was being terminated. Gullit stormed off and went in search of Ken Bates. He never found him and learnt from teletext when he got home that Vialli, the man he had fallen out with, had got his job.

Hutchinson describes these events as enormous for Chelsea. He only slept four hours in two nights and lost almost a stone in weight with the worry. 'At least it was good for my figure if not my stress levels,' he says.

Seriously, Chelsea made a massive decision. Indeed, a brave one. There are not many clubs who would have sacked Gullit in the middle of a season with the team in two cup competitions and still involved in the Championship race.

Chelsea simply refused to be caught out again, Hoddle-style. The Gullit reign lasted eighteen months. Hutchinson says, 'I worked closely with him for that period without ever getting to know him well. He knows how grateful we are for what he did. We wanted it to continue but it couldn't, not on his terms.'

Gullit remains bitter. He has done many interviews since his sacking and none have really explained his true feelings about the situation. A wall has come down. It may have been left to his stunning Italian wife, model Cristina, to take us closer to the truth. She says, 'I am not surprised by what happened at Chelsea. He is impossible to deal with. He thinks he is God and we are all nobodies.' Maybe Gullit got too big for his boots at Chelsea. If that is the case then it is no wonder he was found out. Bates does not tolerate anyone who thinks he is bigger than the club, or him for that matter.

Gullit's wife also revealed a conversation she had with Gianluca Vialli seven months before the sacking. 'Luca told me he was worried about Ruudi, about how he had changed and hardly ever spoke to him, not even to say hello. And how he did not seem to work with the team any more, but just went on his own way.' Again, this backs up what Bates and Hutchinson discovered in their investigations into what was happening behind the scenes, in the dressing room.

Interestingly, Chelsea have already re-written Vialli's deal. He will continue as a player-coach on his same contract until the end of the 1998/99 season. Then, for two years after that, he will concentrate on coaching only, with a reduced salary. The exact contract offered to Gullit. He said no. Vialli said yes.

Was it only down to money that Gullit left? I found it interesting that at Vialli's opening press conference he made it clear that one of his first jobs was to re-build the harmony and spirit in the dressing room. Under Gullit it was most definitely not one hundred per cent. Indeed, one director told me that Ruud had lost the plot with the players.

Bates says of the Vialli decision, 'Like Ruud he has nothing to prove. He was born in a castle, is the son of a multi-millionaire and a rich man in his own right. It is almost the recipe for a playboy. [An interesting choice of word considering the criticism of Gullit.]

'But he has a vast knowledge of football and players and has demonstrated strong man-management skills. He has no learning curve to follow because he is already in-house with a proven backroom staff behind him. Luca has no management experience but neither did Ruud Gullit.

'We appointed Luca because we couldn't wait for Ruud, we couldn't afford him, and a decision had to be made quickly. Had we waited, the pressure internally and externally, from the fans and the media, would have become unbearable. We believe we have got the right man.'

The bottom line is that Chelsea played safe. They had Rix and the rest of the backroom staff in place. Indeed, they had offered them all new, improved contracts regardless of Gullit's decision. They wanted continuity.

Within days of Vialli saying yes, Chelsea signed Danish international Brian Laudrup. His contract with Rangers was about to expire and Gullit had set up the deal, along with Hutchinson. Vialli spoke to Laudrup and the exciting forward was happy to sign. Another £1 million a year-plus arrival. Gullit was unhappy with the execution of the transfer, saying that things had been going on behind his back before he had been told that his job was over.

Chelsea denied that and insisted that Vialli had done nothing wrong. 'Laudrup,' said Hutchinson, 'had said yes before Gullit left and simply confirmed that he would be joining us.'

Bates always described Gullit as a private person. Not someone that he got to know well, or indeed wanted to. Of his managers, Bates only ever became close to John Neal. It is understandable because Neal was his first manager and they had met amid what was a crisis situation for the club. There will always be something special between them. He adds, 'When Hoddle left, we had to continue the upward curve. The same applied after Gullit. Vialli means we can continue with what we have planned without any huge upheaval.'

It is another Chelsea era, the Vialli era. Before Chelsea knew it they had won the Coca-Cola Cup under him. In his first game in charge, Chelsea produced a massive, passionate performance to come from behind and knock Arsenal out of the semi-final. It was a display that showed the players were right behind their new manager. They like him. Vialli is a smashing bloke, although underneath the smile there is a ruthless streak. You do not get to where Vialli is today without being ruthless. The Chelsea players will find out just how ruthless when he starts to build his own team. There will be casualties.

The Coca-Cola Cup Final victory over Middlesbrough, when he dropped himself to let others play – something that went down well with players and directors alike – brought a huge sigh of relief from the boardroom. They wanted him to be successful, to take the pressure off their appointment.

Then there came a run to the final of the European Cup Winners' Cup. Chelsea's form in the Premiership under Vialli may have been as inconsistent as under Gullit but in the Cups there was no stopping them. It is Vialli's intention to make them more powerful in the League, to stabilise a suspect defence and win the Championship. That is Vialli's dream.

So he becomes Chelsea's eighth manager under the Bates rule. All of them have had Chelsea connections; not one of them has been a complete stranger to Chelsea. Will there be another one before this remarkable character retires, quits or does whatever he wants. As I write this he is 66 and still going strong.

Part of the Bates dream is to see Chelsea the Champions of England and playing in the Champions' League. I suspect that it will not be over until that happens. When? Your guess is as good as mine. Will it ever be over for Ken Bates?

9 Will the Real Ken Bates Stand Up?

S O, WHO IS THE REAL KEN BATES? We know all about the stubborn, cantankerous man, the person who fights like a rattlesnake, the man who refuses to take no for an answer and has an answer for everything. But is that the real Bates? Does he enjoy that side of his life? Yes, he loves the crack of argument, the buzz of sensible conversation, the adrenalin of a fight when he knows he must win. God, that has been half of his life, battling for supremacy.

But is it the private life of Bates that reveals the real person? If we look at what he has said and done over the years, there are few times when he bares his soul about the private person. Is the bark camouflaging a much warmer, gentler person inside? I suspect that somewhere in between the two extremes lies the real Bates.

Get to know him and he becomes a much warmer, good-humoured companion. He has a razor-sharp mind and a capacity to out-think anyone.

His enemies have outweighed his friends, or so it seems. The deeper you dig, the more people there are who not only admire Bates but who actually like and indeed love the man.

The enemies have come and gone. The friends have stayed. Loyalty is vital to him. Friendship even more so. He would do anything to beat off an enemy. He would also do anything for a friend.

Chelsea has been his closest friend for almost seventeen years and he has given them everything, huge amounts of his time, a massive slice of his life – and, for that, the club, I hope, are grateful. He has made money out of them, of course he has. There cannot be a person who says that he does not deserve to be paid for what he has achieved. There are things about the club that I, you and anyone else for that matter will not find out. He has his secrets and will probably take them to his grave. Harding for instance swore blind that behind the scenes there are shareholders of Chelsea Village with hidden identities. I gave up the search and came to the conclusion that this is it now with Bates and Chelsea, take it or leave it.

He came in, fought off those who wanted to de-throne him, and set the club up for a bright future. The man deserves an easy run-in now. All the hard games are over: let Mr Chelsea get what he wants without Beecher's Brook looming in front of him every time.

This chapter was the hardest to write, simply because the real Bates is the hardest to find. The battles are there in the club's history and he talks about them with a fierce pride and determination. Talking about himself is not so easy. 'I believe I am a simple, straightforward person,' he says. 'No, you could not call me bland. But I do not believe I have been that controversial either.

'The private Ken Bates is a different person. My image is what you lot created. Bates blasts, Bates bawls, controversial Bates. Tell me the last time I shouted.

'What is controversial? If I say the FA is run by a load of idiots, that is not controversial, that is the truth. If you ask me a question I will give you an honest answer.

'The important thing in my life has been success. We all want to be successful. We all want to win. I have tried to do it in a certain way. In football terms, I do not like a massed defence with a lone striker. That is not me.

'People come to be entertained. Our lot have only turned on the team once, probably in the days of Porterfield. We have come a long way. Winning and entertainment, it is not a bad motto for life, is it?'

There is a defence mechanism inside Bates. If we go back to his teens, we may just find out why. The couple he had called

Mum and Dad were not his natural parents, and it hit him hard to find out. He was sixteen and he vowed that, from that day forward, nothing in his life would hurt him as much.

'If I am honest, finding that out was probably good grounding for the battles of life ahead,' he admits. No one would hurt him again. Not after he discovered that his natural father had deserted him after his real mother had died when he was just eighteen months old. The self-preservation button had been pushed. In public, he has never really taken his finger off it.

He says, 'The couple who brought me up were step-grandparents-in-law. I also had a sister, but she was looked after by another couple and I didn't meet her until she was grown up.' Bates describes the couple who brought him up as 'fantastic people'. The man did not believe that women should go to work, so she scrubbed floors behind his back to earn enough money to send Bates to grammar school.

Life on that council estate in West London taught him the value of money, and also the value of a good education. He gave his five children a good education because, he says, 'education is the one thing that "they" can't take away from you'.

He always loved football and wanted to be a professional. He was born with a club foot but, in 1938, his 'old man' paid £20 cash for an operation on it, the fifth Bates had endured, and it was a success. 'I will always be grateful to him,' he says. Here again is the quality of loyalty that has so affected Bates. If you do something for him, and stay with him, he is fiercely supportive.

'When I was at grammar school I could have joined the Brentford ground staff, but my headmaster wouldn't let me leave school. But I have no regrets about my schooling. It made a big impression on me. My teachers wore collars and ties and had short haircuts and you had to call them sir. If you didn't you got a clip round the ear. It did me no harm. It would do a few hooligans the world of good to go to a place like that.

'Football was always my love. I was the kind of player that is today called a dog. Hard-working, someone who never gave the ball up. I was strong in the tackle. I didn't like letting people past or getting the better of me (another life motto). I got as far as an Arsenal junior, not bad for someone who was born a cripple and who'd injured a leg in a motorcycle accident.'

Bates's first job was for Great Western Region in the ticket reservation office at Paddington Station. After three weeks he was moved upstairs. 'All the guards had to send in their time sheets and I had to work out the averages on a computer. The trouble was that half of the guys didn't send them in, so I ended up making up dummies.'

Bates got bored. After nine weeks he went into the City to be an accountant. He could not go into the army because of his club foot and spent two years in his latest job. 'I learned a lot,' he said. 'It was good grounding for what was to come.'

That was aged eighteen. At twenty-three he bought his first Bentley. At thirty-two he was rich enough to retire, making his money out of a ready-mix concrete business. He sold it after four years for £545,500. He says that he threw himself into work and making money. He had seen his grandparents struggle and had vowed never to be the same. 'In life, nothing is easy. I don't like people who think that the world owes them a living,' he says.

'I've had to fight for everything that I've got. When you start with nothing you are driven by insecurity. At the start you think you might be hit by the bad times again. OK, I may not feel like that now, but I vowed never to take anything for granted, and I never do.

'I wasted my twenties like mad. I didn't have time to socialise. I was driven on by ambition. I went through a period when I didn't work, and I was bored stupid. There was no purpose. I had money but not incentive. There was nothing to get up for in the morning.'

He eventually began a venture capital business, which took him to the Virgin Islands to run an airline. He then bought four sugar farms in Queensland and made a fortune when sugar prices quadrupled. He also developed property in South Africa and has set up a bank in Ireland.

Then came Chelsea and the rest is history. There will always be business deals along the way. In April 1998 he sold his farm in Beaconsfield, Buckinghamshire, a farm that had produced the best ice cream in England, a farm that had 600 magnificent dairy cows, which he sold off at a profit six weeks before the announcement of the BSE crisis. Bates denies that he was tipped off by a huge Chelsea fan, the then Prime Minister, John Major. 'It was all down to those years as an accountant,' he says with a chuckle.

Bates laughs a lot, particularly at his own jokes. He likes to be the centre of attention, dominating dinners or lunches with a tongue that can cut through an opponent at twenty paces. 'I like a sense of humour as long as it is in keeping with mine,' he adds with another grin. 'I can be wicked, but I'm not afraid to use it against myself.

'How do I relax? With friends, a good meal, some nice wine and stimulating conversation. Can I switch off? I enjoy going home to watch television with a glass in my hand. Dave Allen always made me laugh, as did *Steptoe and Son*. I like to laugh. I've been able to switch off and laugh my bollocks off even when I've had the cares of the world on my shoulders.

'I like eight hours' sleep and I have never had a sleepless night.

'I know I am getting older and I have to pace my game a bit now. The older you get, the more you realise your physical limitations. You work around them. But I do not feel 66.

'I always know what is going on around me. The difference today is that I delegate. And I have made sure that the people who are rubber stamping the deals are trustworthy.'

Two of those people whom Bates trusts are David Mellor and Mark Taylor. Mellor does not work for Chelsea and does not take a penny out of the club, but his knowledge of the man is detailed and he offers this insight into Bates the businessman and Bates the friend. 'Ken, in many ways, is a complicated man, but in terms of what he wants out of life he is very straightforward.

'I suspect that he always wanted a big position in football. He owned Oldham and God knows what else, but Chelsea became his spiritual home. It became his life. Not just supporting or owning the club. It is all about creating.

'He doesn't look upon it as Chelsea Football Club, he calls it Chelsea Village. That is what he has created.

'What he has now is far more than a football club. It is a community. He has got tremendous satisfaction out of creating that, and rightly so.

'He is a much gentler person away from the public eye. I recall the first time that I went away with him was on a cruise. He was a delightful host, wonderful company. In public, he is more mellow now because he has achieved most of his ambitions.

'I defend Ken also because he was someone who came into football long before the attraction of television money. He was not someone who walked in and walked off with the money, like so many others.

'He is someone who calls a spade a shovel and he does not suffer fools gladly. In an argument or a fight he does not take prisoners. Take him on at your peril.

'Of course he has made mistakes, although he may not admit them. Take those electric fences. Everyone knew what he was trying to achieve, but he can be his own worst enemy in how he presents things.

'I have found him straightforward in his ambitions and like to think I have always understood him. We have been friends whether I have been an MP, a Minister or just a Chelsea fan. I do not believe we have ever fallen out, although there were times – when he took off my red scarf and jumped on it, for instance – when I was not sure. But that is Ken. You must take him as you find him.

'He can be rude and swear like a trooper. He does like to be the centre of attention and puts you down, but you have to appreciate that beneath all that he is a nice, kind, spontaneous man. He does not believe that he is doing anything more than being heavy handed when he attacks people. He often rings and asks what Penny and I are doing and would we like to pop out for a meal.

'I have never been in business with him, although I find him admirable. But I'll tell you what, if I had to referee one of his fights, there would be times when I would have to stop it and say that Ken was to blame. He knows that.

'People have often accused me of freeloading. That is unfair. I have never had a penny off him or Chelsea. Each season I purchase two expensive season tickets. Besides Bates would not want it or allow it any other way.

'I have always felt with Ken that he believes in one man one vote, and he is the one man. At least you know where he is coming from and where you stand.

'People ask me how long he will keep going. Why should he give up? It depends on how much he retains his strength and health, but there are no slowing up signs yet. Having fought so hard to keep the club, what would life outside it have to offer him? He is not one of the world's naturals when it comes to retirement.

'Chelsea do not exist without him, and he does not exist without them. It is a good partnership.

'It needed a bloody minded man to keep it going through the eighties, and he was that man. He reminds me of Margaret Thatcher. If she had not been such a bloody minded woman, some of the changes that had to be made in Britain would not have been made. She was cussed. Others would not have been so strong. It is a good comparison.

'There will always be moments when you think to yourself that Ken didn't need to say or do that, but he has his own rules. When he began he cleared out all the freeloaders, but there are people that it is sensible to have as guests. He will say I am not having that bugger in and that is that.

'He will insist that the person only wants a free drink. You can argue with him until you are blue in the face, but if he has made up his mind, you will never change it.

'There was one executive club supporter who needed to use the lift to get to his seat. I had the devil's own job of persuading Ken to allow it. You have to accept that is how Ken runs things. He has been successful, so who are we to argue?

'There are people who appear to be terribly nice and then, when you test them out, they are either weak or devious beneath the charm. Ken is the other way around. Beneath the robust exterior there is a decent man with a good heart.

'I like people who declare what they want and then set about getting it. You don't have to keep thinking, Is this bugger trying to sell me a line? I come back to Ernie Clay. On face value, Clay and Bates appear to be similar people, or they did when Ernie was alive. Yet they are two very different people. I was let down by Clay.

'I have no idea whether Ken trusts people and, if so, who those people might be. I do not want to put questions to him that he would not want to ask of someone else. There are parts of Ken's life that I do not understand, and yet what do I want to understand them for? All I want is to go to a football game and enjoy myself. And feel welcome. I have put something into Chelsea because, in their hour of need, I helped them out and Ken, I believe, will always be grateful for that. I have never said that I know Ken like I know some of my friends.

'Ken is also popular, especially with the Chelsea fans. That is where Matthew Harding got it wrong. He thought the fans would turn against Bates. He underestimated the respect they have for him.

'Chelsea have given me more enjoyment than I thought possible. That is not just due to one man, and yet Chelsea would not be where they are today without Ken Bates. His determination, sheer bloody mindedness and his total commitment to the job in hand meant that the club stayed at Stamford Bridge. Lesser men would have thought, God, why am I chucking this money around?

'Those people who have questioned his motives should look at Zola next time they watch Chelsea. It might not have been Zola – it might have been a house in the middle of a housing estate.

'As an MP, I came through a terrible time for football. Mrs Thatcher hated it. She had huge rows with the authorities. It was hard for me working through it. At that stage, Ken Clarke and I were the only ones who enjoyed football. And through all those hard times Bates was raising money and keeping the club afloat.

'Ken certainly doesn't worry about his public image. He likes a drink although I have never seen him drunk. He is like Willie Whitelaw – he believes that white wine is a non-alcoholic drink.'

Mellor enjoys his red wine, and this led to an amazing dinner date that backfired on Bates. The two met at the Dorchester, at Bates's invitation, and he told Mellor that, as he liked red wine so much, he had ordered a special bottle for him. 'It's £124 a bloody bottle,' he announced as the wine waiter approached. Mellor took a sip and went into raptures. 'This is sensational, Ken, thanks so much,' he said. Bates usually only glances at the bill when it is produced, but this time he did a double take. The bill was for more than £2,000. The waiter explained that the bottle he had ordered, and which Mellor had drunk, had in fact been £1,124 a bottle. The hard wooden edge of the wine list had hidden the first digit. Bates realised his mistake, made only a token complaint and paid the bill. It was generous to say the least.

Mellor recalls the evening with amusement, if not pleasure. He says, 'I have only fond memories of my relationship with Ken.

'If I had any influence over him I would attempt to make him more friendly in public. He is not going to change now though. That is Ken Bates.'

Mark Taylor, the solicitor who has worked with him closely since 1992, says, 'Ken is very different socially. The man sitting around a boardroom table is one person, but get underneath the exterior and he is one of the nicest people you could meet. The Ken Bates I know is not the public's image of him at all. I see him playing with my son, laughing, joking and relaxing. I see a kind person, a tough businessman with a soft centre.

'He likes to have confidence in people, and trust. What Ken has done is to transform Chelsea into the second most important club in England, behind Manchester United. Certainly financially. United have a phenomenal base and they began laying that foundation in the sixties.

'Because we didn't have the security of owning our ground, we are ten years behind United. But it won't take us ten years to catch up. In 1992, we were on a par with Crystal Palace – a dilapidated ground and an OK team. We were miles apart from United.

'Now we've got one of the top three or four teams in Britain. Financially the club is very sound and we have one of the top five stadiums in Britain. Ken has brought it from insolvency to where we are today, and that is a phenomenal achievement.

'Between 1982 and 1992, he didn't have the bricks and mortar to achieve anything. Then came the breakthroughs. It is an unparalleled record.

'I am surprised by the mental energy Ken still has. He is the ideas man and yet he doesn't like the details. I can see him being chairman for another twenty years.

'He loves Chelsea, and I have to say I never felt that about Glenn Hoddle or Ruud Gullit. They were never in love with the club, not like the fans or Ken Bates

'I can still see his face when he turned up at his daughter's cottage one night thinking it was just to have a chat and a couple of drinks. It was, in fact, a surprise birthday party and some close friends were there waiting without him knowing. His face was a picture, beaming and smiling. He enjoyed the evening because he was surrounded by people he liked. That is the Bates I know.'

Bates has been married twice. His first marriage lasted for more than twenty years and he was married to his second for thirteen years. Now he lives with Suzannah Dwyer and there are no plans to marry a third time. They are happy together, Most people who know the couple well say that Suzannah has been good for Bates and he admits that he has mellowed.

'Yes, I am more relaxed and mellow, although I am not always allowed to show it. Suzannah and I are very much in love, and let us leave it at that,' he says.

'When we drive to Chelsea's games now, I am happy and contented and look forward to the occasion.'

He has always had a wicked sense of humour. He must have the last word and often a phone call will end with a comment that some people would take to heart, or be offended by. I have grown to expect it and ride it. One former Chelsea player did not appreciate the Bates wit. As he tucked into his pre-match meal, Bates approached and said, 'You know that testimonial dinner we promised you, this is it.' It led to a fierce exchange between the two men, with Bates protesting it was only his sense of humour and the former player refusing to accept such treatment in front of company. Such exchanges have happened before and will certainly happen again.

He likens himself to Sir Winston Churchill. 'He is my hero,' admits Bates, giving us a rare insight into his private thoughts. 'He was a fighter, an intellectual who could paint or lay bricks. He was a man of the people. He said that if something was worth doing, it was worth doing well. I feel like that. And yes, I feel close to the people of Chelsea, and the players. I have always got on well with players.

'We are one big family and I am immensely proud of them.

'I have achieved a lot in my life and there is a sense of satisfaction. But there is more to do. Churchill did not become Prime Minister until he was 65. There are a lot more things I want to achieve yet.

'I want to travel more. I am fascinated by the world. The more you travel, the more ignorant you realise you are. I have not been behind the Iron Curtain and I want to go to India, China and Russia. Parts of South America fascinate me. People fascinate me.

'Have I been lucky? Luck is something bankrupts blame and millionaires never acknowledge. Everyone in this life gets opportunities. Too often the failures do not recognise them or have the guts to take them.

'It is easy to sit on your backside and moan that nothing happens for you. Make it happen. And then fight for it. Fight for what is yours.'

You would never know it now but Bates, for years in his early life, was driven by insecurity. Today he is not someone to open up about his emotions and there is an ever present drawbridge that he does not allow to be lifted. It stems, he says, from the hard times as a child when he fought for everything, tooth and nail. Finding out that his real father was not that bothered about him made him mentally strong. At that time something inside him ticked away, urging him forward. From around the age of sixteen, he vowed that Ken Bates would succeed.

He wanted power, money, success; he wanted to be loved. Inside today's bluster and thunder there is a different Ken Bates. You do not often see him confused or hurt. I was allowed inside these inner feelings on the morning of the European Cup Winners' Cup Final when we sat in the team's plush hotel. We had just finished the last interview for this book when he called me over to another table, switched off my tape recorder and ordered some more coffee.

'I want to talk to you,' he said. He drew his chair nearer and asked me why I thought Matthew Harding had hated him so much, why he had fought so bitterly. Why, indeed, he had forced Bates to respond.

This was a different Bates, an almost vulnerable one, a man looking back while on the verge of his greatest triumph as Chelsea chairman, the club's first European trophy for more than 25 years. There is no question that Bates hated Harding, and still does, but something bugged him, a bug that he will take to his grave. How could someone have hated him so much? I struggled to find the right answers for him, posing questions myself instead of being able to put my finger on why two people can become so loathing of each other.

Throughout my 25 years in national newspapers, indeed throughout my life, I cannot say that I have hated anyone. I have disliked people, have had no respect for them professionally or morally, but to have deep hate is something else.

Bates was forced to hate Harding and it concerns him. While we chatted, a female secretary came over to chat and she stayed for ten minutes, exchanging pleasantries with us before moving on. Bates was both funny and charming and as the girl walked off he predicted a bright future for her inside the club. 'A very bright girl,' he added.

He waved to people, shouted friendly abuse at players and staff, wished Dennis Wise luck and made sure that last-minute arrangements were being dealt with by the right people. 'I have got to make a speech at lunchtime,' he said. 'But the bloke here is superb and we get on so well. I make him laugh.' This was the Bates so many people know – loud, the centre of attention and the man who so often has the last word.

But through the jokes there was the underlying feeling that one question remained unanswered. Harding and his hate. Why did he go to such lengths to de-throne the king when he knew that one day he would sit in the big chair?

Harding was the biggest obstacle to the dream and, while he can no longer bother Bates, it annoys him still. Ah, the dream. The Chelsea dream, the Bates dream.

When did it really start? Was it when he walked into Stamford Bridge in 1982, or was it earlier than that? I suggest that it was long before, years and years prior, when Ken Bates realised that he was born with little and was brought up by people who fought and worked their fingers to the bone for a living and, indeed, to give him the small things he liked.

The Ken Bates dream began then. It was the Chelsea dream that began in 1982.

Bates's whole life has been a dream. To have more, to give himself the trappings of wealth, and he has worked hard and tirelessly to achieve it. He was blessed with a good business brain and a quicksilver mind, and today has the rewards. Yet he is still dreaming – dreaming of the Championship, of completing all the surroundings that mean so much to him, and dreaming of making his club bigger and better than anyone thought possible.

And the dream will never end. Never. There will always be an extension of the rainbow. I suspect he will die dreaming, and what is wrong with that? 'There always has to be another challenge to yourself,' he says. It is true. In my profession of journalism they say the worst thing you can do, after years and years of testing your brain, is to suddenly retire and stop doing anything, stop thinking. Your brain dries up and you become a danger to yourself.

There is no danger of that happening to Bates and the challenges have come thick and fast since he made up his mind that he was going to force his way through.

The first dream would have been to become a professional footballer. He was never good enough and he knew it. Not fast enough, not as skilful as the other players. He was, however, determined – surprise, surprise. He used to tackle harder than the others, foul them and make life as miserable as possible for his opponents. 'I ran myself into the ground,' he says. 'They were not going to beat me without a fight.

'I knew I was never going to make it to the top as a footballer but I have made it to the top as a chairman, and I have made my contribution to football in this country.

'I have always said what I felt, and some people along the way have not liked it. Tough.' That is a typical comment from him. The Newcastle owner and chairman Sir John Hall once said that Bates was a lovely man and someone he admired greatly. 'There is only one thing,' Sir John said. 'He always seems to have this chip on his shoulder.'

It is a chip that will never go away. It has helped him fulfil the dream, to drive him on. He denies it, the chip that is, although it is not difficult to spot, especially in public. In private he is a different person. He is kind and generous and has the ability to drop into different roles 'just like that'. I have grown to like him and respect him. The one thing I will say is that we will miss him when he is gone. 'I am not going anywhere,' he quickly says. 'I am still negotiating with the guy upstairs but we have not agreed terms yet. I don't think that heaven is going to be big enough for both of us.'

Bates is the kind of person who walks into a room to find people nudging each other. 'That is Ken Bates over there,' they say. Journalists will whisper, 'Here he is.' It is a reaction for someone who has demanded just that, a reaction.

'I have designed the ground in the same way as I have designed my life,' he says. 'From the bottom up. Chelsea started with nothing and now look at them – the best ground and the best team. I had nothing when I was a child and I like to think I have fought for all this,' he says, first pointing to the surroundings of the Chelsea Village, and then pointing a finger at his chest.

'We at Chelsea, and that includes me, have to pinch ourselves, remind ourselves of the reality – that we have done so much so quickly.

'I will always be known as Big Bad Bates. It is a title I have lived with ever since I came into football, especially Chelsea. I do not think I am big or bad, just Bates. It would be nice to be known as Big Good Bates, but that doesn't sound right, does it? The people who know me best know what I am like.'

Bates has certainly surrounded himself with people who respect him and want to work for him. He prides himself on knowing all the staff by name, often stopping to talk to them. 'It has taken time to have a team at Chelsea, on and off the pitch,' he says. 'I remember a player in the seventies coming out of the dressing room after a defeat and saying to a staff colleague, "You have to laugh, don't you?" The member of staff felt like belting the player. That has been the attitude I have tried to push into everyone this club employs. Passion and pride. I want staff and players who all care about Chelsea, who want to work and play for us.'

There is certainly passion and pride within the fans for this extraordinary character. The day after Chelsea won the FA Cup in 1997, Bates found himself stranded in the King's Road. The Chelsea celebration coach had passed and the streets were packed – and not a taxi in sight. Bates decided to walk.

It was to prove to be one of the most emotional moments of his life. As he walked towards his destination, Leonardo's Restaurant, he was mobbed by supporters. They came over to shake his hand, thank him, give him gifts and treat him like a president on a walkabout. Bates shook their hands and joked with them. When he got to his lunch date, the restaurant rose as one to applaud him. They knew that this was the man who had saved the club and given Chelsea their pride back. They were winners again.

His lunch took hours as people came in off the street to shake his hand. 'It was,' he recalls, 'a very special time. It is something I will never forget.'

There will always be the minority who dislike Bates, who do not trust him and say, in private, that he has developed Chelsea only for his own means, to make money. There are those who claim that Bates has made a fortune out of the club. 'Totally wrong, and I would like them to try and prove it,' he says. 'If they came forward with some evidence, it would be a start.

'I am the chairman of the club and all people who work hard and are successful get paid. I am no different. But not once have I done anything that has damaged this club, financially or otherwise. There are always a few idiots who want to spoil something good.'

He met one of those 'idiots' face to face on his walkabout through Chelsea after that Cup Final. A stranger rushed up and tried to throw some beer at him and generally abused him. Bates's reaction was typical: he gave chase and was about to thump the person when real Chelsea fans jumped in to stop him. 'I would have bloody belted him too,' says Bates. 'I was impressed with my reaction. It wasn't bad for a pensioner.'

It was an isolated incident in a career that has seen the fans stay loyal to him. As former Chelsea great Peter Osgood says, 'They realise that without him there would be no Chelsea. They will always be grateful.'

Bates adds, 'The good people, the real fans, remember. They remember the bad times, the days when the club almost went bust, the days when we could not attract a decent player.

'I recall trying to sign Richard Gough from Dundee United and we were up against Spurs. Their chairman at the time, Irving Scholar, turned to Gough and said, "What do you want to play for a two-bob outfit like Chelsea for? They might not even be in the league this time next year." He was spot on but it hurt me, it hurt me badly.

'I remember going home that night to think about what Scholar had said. A two-bob outfit, indeed. Not any more. Players now want to play for Chelsea. We are attracting the best, signing the best and paying for the best. Richard Gough would love to play for us now.

'My son once told me never to become blasé because there are so many people whose lives centre around this club, good people, and those are the people I am working for. Those are the people I have built Chelsea for. The fans who can go to the pub in the evening and feel proud; they can have a few drinks by way of celebration, not commiseration.'

After the playing dream failed to materialise, Bates the working man began his rise to the top, street fighting his way around the system, making his money and all the time setting his eyes on the best of everything.

'I am still playing, really,' he says. 'I kick every ball, head every clearance away and score every goal. I would love to have been Zola – darting through, beating players, scoring a great goal and then turning to the crowd and raising my arms in triumph.

'Isn't that everyone's dream who loves football, who always wanted to be the best footballer in the world? I am no different.'

Bates now takes the acclaim from the front row of the directors' box. He often stands up at the end of matches and salutes the supporters shouting out his name. He will even lean over and exchange banter with them. Those are special moments for this man who rarely lets his private image slip through. 'The days I enjoy most now are match days,' he says. 'To drive to London, through Chelsea, and swing into the ground. There it is, the club we have built.

'To go into the directors' area and see people who have been with me all this time and then to watch Chelsea play. Not just to play, but to play wonderful, entertaining football. That is my satisfaction.

'It is the game that is the culmination of the dream. The players in their blue shirts . . . how I wish I was one of them. In a way, I feel I am.'

10 The Future

K EN BATES STILL HAS ENERGY and ambition even though he has achieved what he always intended to do – to make Chelsea great. The dream has come true. 'We have done it,' he says. He has been thoroughly lifted by the experience.

'There were some hairy moments along the way and who knows what would have happened had we not kept it going? I cannot keep repeating that I love this club and I have never once used it to fight for my own needs.

'I took over the debts and for ten years did not take a penny out of the club. In 1992 I began being paid £120,000 a year but today I no longer receive a salary.

'There was never a time when I thought I would bail out. Never. We had some tough fights but won them all. It was never plain sailing and no one can accuse us of being boring.

'We have cut some ribbons and we will cut a lot more along the way.'

Us? We? Bates deliberately uses these pronouns because he is rightly proud of the people he now has around him. The people who will carry the dream on and on when he eventually retires. Will that ever happen? I doubt it somehow. The people he has handpicked, the staff he can trust, do not think so either.

'We are a good team on and off the pitch,' he says. Bates has around him men like Colin Hutchinson, the chief executive, and Alan Shaw, the company secretary. 'Alan was the first outside employee we brought in,' explains Bates. 'He broke the mould. There was a very tight clique running the club and Alan had a hard first year settling in. Now I call him the rock of Gibraltar. He is the person who sweeps up all the mess, if there is any. You would not perhaps recognise him but he does a valuable job and he is vital to us.

'They are the ones who make it tick. Like Yvonne Todd. She was the finance director and she is now in charge of training staff and investment, plus auditing. When we didn't have two bob to rub together she kept the creditors at bay. We used to say that the area manager of our former bank was secretly in love with her. I am sure it is not true but he never missed an opportunity to take her out to lunch. She never failed to come back with the money or an agreement.

'Yvonne never told me when we did have money in the bank, otherwise we would have spent it. If we wanted a new player or a roof on somewhere she told us whether we could or not. At one stage we couldn't pay our VAT, but Yvonne sorted it out. The great thing about her is that when she promised people something she always delivered, and they respected her for that. There has to be trust. Her word was good enough. She has been a loyal servant of this club. Yvonne does projects that you never hear about, but if they were not done then things would not run so smoothly.

'Then, take Stuart Thompson, one of the directors of Chelsea Village. He ran a company called Silver Service before they sold out to Heinz. He had a family trust and he was the first to buy £500,000 worth of shares when I was looking for the ten people to invest. Harding was the second person I met. When it was tough, and Harding was giving us a hard time, Stuart borrowed a million to subscribe to more shares. It has paid off because he has now doubled his money, but the fact of the matter is that he was there when we needed him. It was a joint decision he took with his wife, who is also Chelsea potty.

'Running a football club often requires swan-like behaviour – on the surface, all is calm, smooth and serene but, underneath the water, the feet are going like crazy.

'That is happening at all football clubs, probably more so at Chelsea because we are moving so quickly, doing things so fast. The speed is rapid and some people do not appreciate what is hitting them.

'That is one of the problems we have with the council because they cannot cope with the changes. Behind the scenes we are moving fast, too fast for the council.'

Other members of the loyal Bates team are Michael Russell, the finance director, Mark Taylor of course, a non-executive director, Chris Benson, Peter Price, the catering manager, Chris Gleeson, the facilities manager and Chris Manson, the merchandise manager. 'We are an empire now,' says Bates.

The players, too, are important to him. He has already said that his relationship with players, generally, has been good. Bates likes to be liked. One Chelsea player who took an instant liking to him and has held that relationship ever since is Dennis Wise, the captain, who was signed by Bobby Campbell. Wise, currently playing the best football of his career, has been loyal to club and chairman all the way.

He says of Bates, 'I like and respect the bloke, yes, even love him, and I'm not ashamed to say it.

'When I first signed for Chelsea I turned up in a track suit and my greeting to him the first time we met was, "Hello, Batesy". I recall Andy Townsend arriving in a lounge suit and saying, "Good morning, chairman." Ken Bates liked my cheek from that day and has liked me ever since.

'I don't think people realise just how much he has done for the club. We know now that there would not be a Chelsea without him. He has done so much, turned the club around completely.

'At one stage he took terrible stick, especially when the Matthew Harding thing was at its peak. He was under pressure then, both as a person and as a chairman. It hit him hard, but he stuck to what he believed was right.

'I remember how he treated me when I first joined. The contracts had been signed and then Wimbledon owner Sam Hammam said the club couldn't pay me what they owed me. It was a fair bit, and Sam said that I would have to stay at

Wimbledon. I was sick, and told Ken. He asked how much it was and, when I told him, he just said that Chelsea would put it on my contract with them. It was a generous thing to do, and I have never forgotten that.

'He didn't have to do it but it made me realise how much the club wanted me. I respect the bloke for what he has done here and the fact that he has kept going when so many people were jumping on the bandwagon to push him out or criticise him. Those people can't say anything now. Look at the club. He is Mr Chelsea.

'People haven't liked him because he has gone for what he wants. There is nothing wrong with that. The club has got bigger than I ever thought it would. I suspect that Ken Bates always knew, deep down, that the breakthrough would come. The ground is fantastic and we are not far away with the team. We are winning things.

'My girlfriend, Clare, and I have been out for meals with Ken and Suzannah. Like I say, I love them. He calls me his little son. I don't mind, even if the chaps (the other players) take the mickey. They know how I feel about him. They should realise that without him they would not be here. None of us would.'

Wise is right about one thing – Bates will not stop until the club are right at the top. And there will always be other dreams. Bates adds, 'There is still a lot to do, and we have the people to do it.'

Apart from the facilities offered by the hotel and restaurants inside Chelsea Village, Chelsea now have a hugely successful megastore, a mail-order firm, their own wine brand and, in the near future, there is to be a museum, another hotel with 131 rooms (the first floor will be in place by the start of the 1998/99 season), a new main entrance incorporating a shop, eight residential apartments, a car park at the back of the stadium, a 50,000-square-foot sports and leisure centre to be run in conjunction with a well-known company, and Chelsea Railway Station, to improve rail links.

When you consider that the Southern Complex cost £30 million, the West Stand £24 million and the North Stand £14 million, it is not difficult to understand why Bates is proud.

'They said people would not invest in us, because of me,' he reminds us.

The West Stand is still to be finished, with its four tiers, exclusive boxes, an exhibition hall and sixteen suites overlooking the pitch. The money for all of this is already on deposit via the Euro-bond. Chelsea do not have to borrow a penny.

Is that all? 'No, things are happening all the time,' says the man who made it all possible. 'The wine we sell under our name is Pouilly Fume, which I drink at home and we serve in the boardroom. It is not the paint stripper other clubs give.' Chelsea also have their own brand of champagne. You will be able to buy the wine and champagne at the nine restaurants that will soon be open at Stamford Bridge.

He wants Chelsea cheese, and ice cream (two of his favourite loves), and jams, and yoghurts. The ideas come thick and fast to him. 'What about a Chelsea hamper, like Harrods do?' He is serious about everything now. 'A company has just paid £75,000 to use their coffee in our restaurants and bars. They can see what is going on here,' he says proudly.

'Our wine will probably bring in half a million a year and that is one player's wages. Our club call is the best in football. I like everything to be the best.'

Dare anyone say that the Chelsea of 1998 is not better than the Chelsea of the seventies and eighties? One supporter did, and got a typical Bates retort. 'You not only look like a prat, you act like one too. Come and see me after the game and two security guards will throw you out and someone else will piss in your pocket. Fuck off.'

He has not come this far to be told that it was better before. Those who do not like him are those who have not been able to keep pace with this character, the like of which football will not see again. The tickets are priced high at Stamford Bridge, but the facilities and the team are worth paying for, according to the chairman.

Bates says, 'All those years ago I showed a model of my dream to anyone who came into my office or was interested. There were not many who believed that it was possible. All clubs have a golden age, and I believe this is ours. Leeds had it, so did Liverpool; United are in theirs and, now, here comes Chelsea. Nothing goes on forever, but you must enjoy it while it lasts, build the rock foundations to carry the weight of failure when it comes, and then be strong enough to come back again and again.'

Mellor, head of the government's task force as well as a Chelsea fan, looks at Chelsea's future like this, as a business and an enjoyment. 'The great thing for Ken is that he has achieved what he wanted to achieve without having to depend on money brought in by a Matthew Harding-type person.

'Bates has been lucky in that football has become fashionable. Chelsea's prices are high but Ken can charge what he believes are the right seat prices because fans will buy, indeed they are demanding tickets. I pay £800 for my season ticket. There are some high prices and I suspect that one day I will have to put on my task force hat and have a word with him about it. But there are sections around Stamford Bridge that are affordable to the bedrock fan. I expect that in the coming years he will increase the price of the tickets at the top end faster than those at the other end of the scale.

'The club is generating an awful lot of money. It has an extraordinarily high wage bill because of the foreign stars who have arrived, but it is more than coping. That is down to good management on and off the pitch.

'I never thought Ruud Gullit would go. In fact, I would have wagered a substantial amount that he would have stayed. But that is football. Chelsea believed that they could not progress as they wanted with him, and who can argue with decisions made by Ken Bates?

'But you are talking to someone who has called things wrong before – when John Major was appointed I thought that the Conservative Party was a band of brothers. I do believe that Chelsea's future is bright. They appear to be on a roll. Will the bubble burst, as we have seen so many times at this club? No, I don't think it can.

'I think the climate of football favours Chelsea. With our new facilities, the catchment area we are in and the fact that the top names want to come to London, we are booming.

'The Bosman ruling means that top players are more readily available. We believe that we are in the top ten clubs in the world and I have no doubt that the phone lines are hot with agents asking Chelsea about players who they know are available.

'It is all part of the rise and rise of Chelsea, although everyone knows that we still have quite a way to go.

'There is no doubt that Chelsea is built on a firmer foundation than some other clubs. A lot of money is being spent in areas where a lot of prudent businesses would not spend so freely. The worry is that the football bubble might burst. Ken Bates is a good businessman. My guess is that in five years' time Chelsea will be even better placed than we are today.

'I relate it to one of those players I watched on one of my first visits to Fulham all those years ago. I saw that young black defender and thought what a great future he had. I was proved right over Paul Parker. The same prediction goes for Chelsea. We have a very bright future.

'Chelsea have a fashionable image as well as being an outstanding football club. We already have Zola, Di Matteo, LeBoeuf, Le Saux, and more will follow. Those players must love it at Chelsea. Take LeBoeuf. He had no recognition in France. He must think he has found paradise, living in London and playing for Chelsea. Bates says that Zola is one of the sweetest people he has met.

'I am getting more enjoyment than I have ever had before. The bubble burst too quickly in the seventies. We won two cups and then things went away quickly. The club and the team then had a cavalier approach. It is far more professional now.

'Chelsea has arrived at this point because of Ken Bates. Without his determination and sheer bloody mindedness, his total commitment, Chelsea would not even be at Stamford Bridge. We would probably be talking about them in the past tense.

'Ken is totally stimulated by what he is doing. He feels he has reached the sunlit upland. There is another peak for him because he is full of ideas. I hope that one day he rests his brain, and he must be careful not to overreach himself. But that is territory that only he knows.

'Ken feels he has cracked it, rather than having things to crack. He feels he is on the home straight. Good luck to him. Chelsea Football Club owe him a lot. Everything, really.'

Taylor says, 'The whole thing is a remarkable story. Chelsea are now self-perpetuating. There have been different eras but now we go on. What Gullit did was sensible. In the first year, he obtained older pros, then in came the younger ones, like Poyet, Babayaro, Granville and Le Saux. Now Luca will take us on again.

'The club runs itself, with Ken centre stage. He knows what is going on and has his input into everything. He has to like, trust and admire all of his staff. However, he is not a blood brother of any. For instance, I don't believe that he has ever been to Colin's home. Nor does he socialise with the manager or players, apart from the obvious functions.

'He was under a huge strain at one stage, and he came through. I can't see him ever retiring.

'Ken Bates is in control – at Chelsea there is only one man to answer to. I think that is one thing that Matthew Harding could never understand – how Ken is loved by so many people at Chelsea. He never came to terms with that.'

The Ken Bates dream culminated in 1998 by Chelsea winning the Coca-Cola Cup Final at Wembley against Middlesbrough and reaching and winning the European Cup Winners' Cup Final. A great cup double and it came within weeks of Bates sacking Gullit and replacing him with Vialli.

On the pitch, the 1997/98 season was significant and successful, a move right up the ladder of success for the club. We were in Stockholm for the European Cup Winners' Cup Final when he looked back on a successful season with huge pride. As he sipped his coffee, the Beard said, 'When the season began back in August, hell that seems such a long time ago because so much has happened, there was expectancy in the air. We had won the FA Cup, which was a significant breakthrough in our history, and more new players had arrived.

'Of course we expected a successful season. We wanted to grow and grow. The first match of the season was at Coventry. We were so superior it was embarrassing, but we lost 3–2. In a way, I now think that it was not such a bad thing, although I would never have admitted it at the time. The defeat brought a few people back down to earth. They realised that we couldn't simply stroll through the season.

'There were things going on off the pitch all the time, as there are today. We were working at breakneck speed to get the South Stand open. The council were helpful although at the same time we were in discussions about building the pedestrian link to Fulham Broadway Station.

'I also wanted to knock down the old West Stand and start building the new one. The deal we did allowed us to build the lower tier and leave the upper to be sorted out later. So all those things were going on as we approached the start of the season. It was exciting and stimulating.

'It was hectic. We also put a new revolutionary pitch in and so, all in all, we had a lot to do. We also had the new players, like Tore Andre Flo and Gustavo Poyet, who are going to be part of our long-term future. We also signed Ed De Goey in goal. We lost Scott Minto, Erland Johnsen went home to Norway and Craig Burley was sold to Celtic. All in all, we did well by the Bosman transfer system. We have come to terms with Bosman while other clubs have struggled to use it properly.

'The great thing about football is that you can never celebrate for long. You win something and go on to the next. You have to forward plan all the time. I remember that great story about Sir Alf Ramsey after he had won the Championship with Ipswich. The Cobbold brothers, who loved to celebrate and enjoyed a drink as we know, approached Alf the next day and invited him out to celebrate the Championship. He told them to fuck off because he had to watch the reserves. Football is like that. It is a cycle, it never ends.

'A number of people say to me, "The summer is here, you can have a rest now." But the close season is often busier than the season itself.

'I will never be satisfied. If you become satisfied, you become complacent – and that is the first step downhill.

'People also say that I have achieved what I set out to do. Yes, we are stable and secure. But we only finished fourth in the League and got knocked out of the FA Cup in the third round. Also, the injuries we picked up during the season revealed our lack of depth.

'There is still a lot to do. I would not say I am delighted with what has happened this season, despite the cup wins. For instance, we should have qualified for the Champions' League.

'We can point at our inconsistency in the League, but I also blame some strange team selections by Ruud Gullit. We played at Everton in a game we had to win. Zola and Wise were fit and wanted to play. Ruud refused. They were not even on the bench but sat, instead, behind us in the directors' box. We were amazed. We lost 3–1. We should have won that game – Everton were there for the taking. That was the start of our decline in the League.

'We remembered little things like that when the dispute with Ruud came up. There was also the team he sent out against Manchester United in the FA Cup. I think he finally took leave of his senses over that one. We could not believe it in the directors' box when we got the team sheet.

'When he finally made the changes, with twenty minutes to go, we scored three goals.

'So, when the wages thing came up, we decided to bite the bullet. Essentially he was sacked because we could not afford to meet his demands but other, not insignificant things were perhaps also taken into account. When Colin Hutchinson came to me and told me that we had a potential problem with Ruud, I began to make investigations and discovered little things that worried me. You put all those together when making a big decision.

'I recall inviting him out to lunch once and he said that he couldn't make it because he had to go to the bank. On another occasion he said he was too busy. I thought to myself, There's something wrong here. You don't snub your boss twice, do you? Especially when the subject for conversation is a possible new contract.

'Unlike some chairmen, I do not have a quick emotional reaction. I store it in the computer. You paint a picture and build up the character in your mind.

'People have said that I often come back months later with something that was mentioned nine months ago. I never forget.

'I appreciate that on the outside the decision to sack Ruud Gullit appears to have been total madness. We had to do it. Colin Hutchinson did his homework and we had a smooth baton change with Gianluca Vialli. No one is bigger than the club, and this proves it.

'When the time comes for me to hand over my baton, I will. But at the moment there is no one running up behind me for a changeover.

'Another feature of the season was the peculiar injuries, serious injuries, we suffered without playing in games. Poyet was out with a training injury, as was Babayaro, who is a talented young man, I'm sure, but we've hardly seen him yet. He also got a kick at Spurs, which didn't seem serious but it kept him out for some time. We missed Poyet because he is a class player.

'It hasn't been a good season for injuries, but we've not shouted and screamed about our bad luck, we've just got on with it. At Newcastle, Frank LeBoeuf played for forty-five minutes because he had to – we had no one left.

'I think this season we have discovered what we are capable of. It has been great to win two cups, and those successes have been significant, but I wouldn't say we have realised our full expectation. But we have finished higher than ever in the Premiership, and not even Hoddle had that success. His record was eleventh, fourteenth and eleventh. And Ruud didn't do that much better in the League. Now we are fourth – and we want to finish first.

'Let us not forget that we have won three trophies inside twelve months. People now look upon us in a different light and there is more respect, but we still lack the killer instinct. We have to kill-off teams.

'We also give silly goals away and our defence has to be strengthened. But, like everything else with us, it is all being put right. We are capable of beating anyone on our day, but that is no good if you are still losing silly matches.

'I don't think it helped when the Premier League offered us no help with fixture congestion. Peter Leaver, chief executive of the Premier League, offered us help, but it never came. Nothing. We asked clubs if our games could go back to Sunday after a European week. Most helped, but some didn't. They should have been ordered.

'Leeds, for instance, had to be told to move. They wanted to play us on the Monday when we were in Europe on the Thursday! If a club is playing in the Cup Winners' Cup then they should play on the Sunday, with a home game, not told to travel half the length of the country. You are going to lose because you are knackered. It is unfair and has to be corrected. I will continue to fight for those things on behalf of football, not just Chelsea.

'For us, these are unquestionably exciting times. We will sell out of season tickets for next season. People want to see us play.

'We last won in Europe in 1971. That should have been the start of something big. Instead, the people who ran the club let it fall to pieces. A good side was broken up and the club was brought to its knees. The difference, twenty-seven years later, is that we will go from strength to strength.

'There are no more obstacles off the pitch as far as I can see, no hurdles to jump. As long as we all paddle the same way then Chelsea can just go one way. Up. Up.'

Ken Bates even has a new slogan for the club he bought, saved and re-built: 'Chelsea, a Way of Life.'

Why not? That is exactly what it has been for Ken Bates for the last sixteen years. The Ken Bates dream turned into a way of life.

11 The Season that Proved Everything

AS KEN BATES DROVE ALONG the M40 and M42 motorways towards Coventry on 9 August for the start of the 1997/98 season, there was only optimism in the air. Between conversation with Suzannah and listening to classical music on his CD player, he thought about a lot of things. His club, the new season, the players Chelsea had signed, the future; he thought about how close Chelsea were to becoming the best club in the country. It was a lovely summer's day, hot sunshine, blue skies and just a slight breeze. It felt good. Bates was happy and contented as his Bentley swung off the M42 and into Coventry. There was no question that all his problems were now behind him. It was just football now, and the only hurdles to jump would be those that sport threw up. He thought about his health and realised he felt good. Not bad for an old one. Yes, it was going to be a good season. He was convinced of that as he strode into the Coventry boardroom, shook hands with their directors, nodded at a few familiar faces and ordered a glass of champagne. It tasted good – the taste of success.

Ninety minutes later, Chelsea had lost. They had played Coventry off the pitch with some breathtaking, attacking football. But, once again, the defending let them down. Every time Coventry hit the ball long towards centre forward Dion Dublin, they looked vulnerable. New goalkeeper Ed De Goey played well enough, although this was not an inspiring performance by any means. They had even taken the lead through Frank Sinclair, who celebrated by dropping his shorts around his ankles and was subsequently fined and warned by the Football Association. The journey home for Bates was not so enjoyable. 'I knew we had played well, but we'd lost,' he says. 'I'd had enough of such displays in the past. "Good old Chelsea," people would say, "entertaining, yes, but they'll not win anything." This reputation is something that I had vowed to kill off.

'Some of our football at Coventry was outstanding but, yet again, the defending was poor. I remember thinking to myself as we drove home that maybe we still needed to buy top-class defenders. If our ambition is to win the League then we are going to need the best at the back. You cannot give goals away, stupid goals at that, if you want to be considered the top club side in English football. And that is exactly what I want.'

Chelsea's defence on the opening day was a flat back four comprising Sinclair, Frank LeBoeuf, veteran Steve Clarke and young Danny Granville – Graeme Le Saux was not fit. Michael Duberry had still not recovered from his serious leg injury. It was a defence that did not look particularly strong on paper, and so it proved. Defending had been Chelsea's Achilles' heel for seasons and, on the evidence of that first day of the 1997/98 season, it appeared that this was still the case. Dublin helped himself to a hat trick, the winner coming in the closing seconds after a typical mistake in Chelsea's six-yard box. 'I felt a mixture of annoyance and depression when they scored that late winner,' recalled Bates. 'We had played some good football and yet lost. OK, I did get that "not again" feeling.'

A week later, on a Sunday afternoon in Yorkshire, Chelsea smashed newly promoted Barnsley 6–0. Gianluca Vialli, ignored for the opening game, scored four times. At the end of the game, as Vialli walked off to a standing ovation from Chelsea's large and loyal following, he got a hug and pat on the head from manager Ruud Gullit. It was an interesting and significant moment. Let us first examine the relationship between these two legends of world football.

Gullit had signed Vialli and then, it is said, became jealous of his popularity with the supporters. Football fans are fickle people but if they like you, they like you. They took to Vialli instantly, chanting his name and demanding his selection. At Chelsea's new impressive megastore, just off the King's Road and close to the main entrance of Stamford Bridge, Vialli shirts outsold any other player's, including that of Gullit himself. The other players also liked Vialli. He was a gentleman who had time for them, did not react to the dressing room banter, as Gullit did, and always had time for the young players, passing on advice and encouraging them on the training ground.

Throughout the 1996/97 season, Gullit's first in control, no one at the club could understand Gullit's handling of Vialli. Particularly the directors. Here was a world-class player and yet the manager would not select him regularly. Long before the break came, the Chelsea board had discussed the deteriorating relationship between Gullit and Vialli. 'Gullit treated him like shit,' says Bates. I suppose that is one way of putting it.

The relationship fell to such an extent that by the time the Cup Final came, and the 2–0 victory over Middlesbrough, the two of them were hardly talking. Gullit put Vialli on the bench and only brought him on for the final few minutes. Significantly, Vialli waved a goodbye to the Chelsea fans at the end of the game. 'I thought it was my last appearance for Chelsea,' Vialli admitted. 'I did not want to go but I could see no real future for me at the club. I celebrated with the club and the other players at the banquet after the game but it was tinged with sadness.'

After his four goals at Barnsley, Vialli was kept in the side for the next game, a 2–0 midweek win at London rivals Wimbledon. But for the next match, at home to Southampton, he was out again. It was to be the story of his season until the dramatic happenings in February 1998. Vialli, at the time he scored his four goals at Barnsley, and certainly in the summer of 1997, would not have put any money on becoming Chelsea manager.

It was just a twist, certainly the biggest twist of all, in the season that proved everything at Chelsea. Gullit's sacking and Vialli's promotion certainly proved that anything can happen at this famous football club, and it usually does. 'No, nothing surprises me any more,' says Bates. 'I would not have thought, driving away from Coventry after our first game, that we would have a new manager by February. But after what I have been through in my life, certainly in football – certainly at Chelsea, you are ready for all eventualities. At the back of your mind you have this little mechanism that switches on in a crisis. I certainly take pride in being able to react and to sort things out quickly. It is probably because I have always had a very active mind. Yes, even at my age. The bones may be getting older, the brain is still alert.'

Chelsea beat Southampton 4–2, won another London derby, this time 3–2 at Crystal Palace, and set off on the European Cup Winners' Cup trail with a 2–0 home win over Slovan Bratislava with goals from Roberto Di Matteo and Granville who, at £200,000 from Cambridge, was proving to be a superb find amongst all the big names and big earners at the club. Just as Chelsea and Bates were gearing up for the expected European and English onslaughts, they lost at home to Arsenal in another Sunday game. When Arsenal's veteran left back Nigel Winterburn smashed home a rare goal, from 25 yards out, it was just another reminder that Chelsea were still not ready, indeed did not have the consistency, to beat the best when it mattered. 'I felt then that it was going to be another "nearly" season in the League,' said Bates. 'The signs were that against the best teams we still did not have good enough defenders. Even at that stage, Colin Hutchinson and I were looking into the future. You have to plan way ahead in football. Not once in my career in the game have I felt that I have cracked it, certainly not on the pitch.

'As you probably know by now my dream is for Chelsea to become the biggest and best club side in Europe. In defence I knew, even at that early stage of the season, that we were still not good enough. Going forward, our play often had me on the edge of my seat, bursting with pride, because I felt happy for the fans, who always love to be entertained, but at the back it was a completely different story. It is not something you mention to the manager, but it is discussed in private and at board meetings.'

Inconsistency has been Chelsea's downfall ever since Bates took control. Hopes have been raised and then dashed by the various sides. 'There have been great moments, frustrating times, and some months when you wondered why you were doing it at all,' he says.

'Under John Neal we played some good football and yet always fell short of what he wanted, and what the club expected. Chelsea's fans have always demanded entertainment and I have been aware of that.

'Every decision I have made, every manager employed and player signed, has been done with success in mind. I am a Chelsea fan, although people will not always believe that. I have always wanted the best and it is only now that I – no, that we are able to bring the supporters what we feel is the best.

'I will not rest until Chelsea are Champions of England and playing in the Champions' League. It is where this club deserves to be and where, on my first day, I vowed I would take them. I can remember walking into the ground for the first time and thinking how shabby it looked. It did not have the style of a big, successful club.

'Where was the feeling of greatness? Well, a lot of work has gone into producing that feeling. On my first day I made the promise to myself that one day Chelsea would be great. It is easy to say now, I know that, but look back over the years and no one can surely say that I have not kept that promise.

'Even those people who dislike me cannot say that Ken Bates has not striven to give Chelsea back their greatness. I suppose there have been times when people needed convincing. That, too, has taken a while. It has been worth it.

'How many times have I heard people say that Ken Bates talks bollocks, he will never do it, Chelsea are finished, they will never mix with the best? I listened and laughed, because I had faith.

'I wanted a winning side, not a flash-in-the-pan outfit that wins one week and disappears the next. I did not want a side who could turn it on against the best and then fail against the smaller clubs.

'Until recently we were still fifteen years behind the

Manchester Uniteds of this world because we wasted so much time fighting property spivs, then dealing with the bloody megalomaniac Matthew Harding. He held me back with that power struggle. Had he put one and one together and even come up with one and a half he could have had all he wanted. But that is history.

'My job has been to secure this club and to provide the funds for the managers to buy the best players available. Over the years we have never fought shy in the transfer market.

'Now we are out there in Europe, buying the best, competing with the top nations. Any club in Europe now knows that if Chelsea want someone, we will fight bloody hard to get him, and we are not scared to offer a few bob.'

Chelsea have bought throughout Bates's reign. Most managers have been told they have money to spend and he has backed them in the transfer market. Under Neal, Bates travelled the country looking for bargains and unknowns who could be turned into stars. He went with Neal to watch Kerry Dixon at Reading, travelled to Scotland to spy on Pat Nevin, and Neal admits, 'The old boy was often a bloody nuisance but you couldn't knock his enthusiasm. I would say, "I'm just off to Scotland to watch so and so," and he would say quickly, "I'll come." It was hands on and I admired him for it.'

Bates recalls, 'The turnover of players has been huge and I daren't think exactly how many we have bought, sold, got rid of, cried over, laughed with and made mistakes over. People have criticised me for interfering but I say to them one thing – prove it.

'I have given my managers support, money, paid them bloody well and only acted to make changes when I felt it would benefit Chelsea Football Club, certainly not Ken Bates.

'I have often felt like coaching them, treating them when they have been injured and giving the team talks but that, surely, is only natural. I have always been a dreamer, still am, who is determined to make his dreams come true.

'In the front row of the directors' box I kick every ball, head every cross, clear every threatening pass, score every goal. I love Chelsea.'

After Neal, the player turnover continued under John Hollins and right down the line until Bates and his trusted chief executive Colin Hutchinson made a big company decision – to engage Glenn Hoddle. Bates says, 'Colin and I sat down and decided that it was about time we moved away from being just another club in London.

'We were fed up with being linked with the likes of Crystal Palace and QPR. We had to break out. We had to become big. Bigger players, bigger crowds and bigger results. The Hoddle signing was significant, a turning point in the club's history.

'It was time for Chelsea to stop being the bridesmaid and start being the bride. It was time for us to start going on a European honeymoon. A honeymoon that would last, not fade away after a couple of years. Yes, it is back to the inconsistency thing again, that has always been a bugbear.'

Hoddle brought Gullit and Mark Hughes and Bates was impressed. 'So were the fans,' he says. 'Here were two players with massive reputations, two players to help us win things. It was the start of a new platform.'

Chelsea, however, were still too inconsistent. 'We got to the Cup Final and two semi-finals under him but we didn't pull up any trees in the League. When he went, I didn't spill any tears because I knew there was still more developing to do, on and off the pitch. He had started the playing revolution but was never going to finish it. His job had been done and there was new ground to tread, new decisions to make.'

Again, it was that damn thing inconsistency that haunted Chelsea as they continued through the 1997/98 season. After that home defeat by Arsenal, they drew 2–2 at Manchester United and beat Newcastle at home 1–0 with a goal from a very impressive signing, Gustavo Poyet. He, however, was soon to be injured and ruled out for months, a wicked blow to Chelsea's hopes.

A European victory in Bratislava sent them into round two of the Cup Winners' Cup and on Sunday 5 October they went to Liverpool for what was surely going to be as good a test as any on their improved line up. Again Vialli was on the bench and Chelsea lost 4–2 after a disappointing, sluggish performance. It was no surprise. Once more Chelsea had failed to convince the fans, and the large TV audience, that they were ready to move to the top of the tree. That has been the trouble with the club. If you are away from a radio or television and hear that Chelsea have lost, you are not surprised. It is a feeling that has bugged Bates and he will not rest until he has put it right.

Chelsea spilled into their most frustrating form of the season. Gullit began the Coca-Cola Cup campaign by fielding weakened teams, a few first team players plus a sprinkling of reserves. They drew at home to Blackburn and won on penalties. Then, in the next round, Gullit did the same, but a late goal by Jody Morris sent them through. At that stage you did not know whether they really wanted to progress. Bates says, 'You leave the selection to the manager. My attitude has always been to win anything that's going.'

A 1–0 home win in the Premiership was followed by a 3–2 European defeat at Tromso in Sweden, in appalling conditions. When the side arrived to inspect the pitch the night before it was snowing heavily and huge plastic sheets covered the surface. Gullit pulled a section of it up to discover ice, rock hard ground and snow spilling under the protection. 'We can not play on this,' he said. 'It will not be a game of football.'

The game did go ahead and only two goals from Vialli saved Chelsea from a heavy defeat. When you look back it was Vialli who kept them in the competition. Bates recalls, 'They were two of the most important goals of the season. I could hardly see Luca when he got them, the snow was so bad, but we were grateful.'

Vialli was even better in the return, getting a hat trick in a 7–1 victory. It was his second hat trick of the season, following his four at Barnsley, and easily made him the club's top scorer, despite Gullit's handling of him. Vialli had come back for the season in determined mood. He had cut out smoking, lost weight and admitted that making love to his girlfriend helped his football. Bates says, 'The bloke showed a lot of character. He knew he was under pressure because of the relationship he had with Gullit, but he responded positively. It was the reaction of a true professional.'

Despite the inconsistency, a defeat at Bolton and then victory at Villa, Chelsea stayed in the top five. Gullit kept commenting how amazing it was that teams were losing games and yet still had a chance of the Championship.

Bates had never been in a position like this before. No side under his sixteen-year control had possessed such quality and hope. He says, 'We all know about the changes in football and we like to think we have been ahead of those changes.

'It was Chelsea who asked Gullit to become our manager and with him came the new approach, the European contacts and the way of life that English footballers are discovering is good for them.

'We also like to think that we are one of the best clubs in England in dealing with the Bosman transfer ruling. People ask where the money comes from. How much would the likes of Di Matteo, Zola and LeBoeuf have cost had we signed the same type of player from within our home game? We could not have done it. We now have a huge network of people working within Europe for us.

'And don't give me that crap about foreign players stopping the progress of our young ones. The local kids all want to come here because they want to learn from the stars. They will be the Chelsea of tomorrow, when we are the best in the land.

'In the past we have had good sides, winning sides, but not consistently good, winning sides. We have had Jack the lads, players who only flirted with what this club is now all about. We are a professionally run organisation with players who take their work seriously.

'And since Matthew Harding died there are no splinter groups within the club. We are all pulling together. Someone said when we got to the Cup Final against Middlesbrough that we should dedicate the victory to Harding. "Why?" I asked. "One of our turnstile operators died just before that final, why not dedicate it to him?" Do I miss Matthew Harding? Are you serious?'

All the changes began with Hoddle of course. The dietitians, the masseurs, the faith healing – the new way forward. Gullit changed it slightly and relaxed the rules. He said, 'What is the point of ordering a player not to eat this and that when behind my back he is tucking into bangers and mash. There has to be a sensible approach.'

By the time Everton were beaten 2–0 at Stamford Bridge, with goals from Dennis Wise and Gianfranco Zola, Chelsea were third, and behind the scenes talks were beginning with Gullit over a new contract. When they beat Derby 4–0 in one of their best performances of the season, with Zola getting a hat trick, no one would have guessed that Gullit's reputation, and future, were beginning to be doubted by Colin Hutchinson and Bates.

Chelsea were second and flying again. Derby was followed by the 6–1 destruction of Spurs at White Hart Lane with Flo getting a treble this time. A 4–1 win at Sheffield Wednesday made them one of the most dangerous and attractive sides in the land. Gullit spoke glowingly of his players after each game and gave the impression that nothing was troubling him.

That was Gullit, of course. As cool as you like on the outside and not a trace of emotion. No one would have known that he was being pressed on a contract, no one would have known that he had been angering Hutchinson by refusing to discuss a new deal. He certainly would not have known that Bates was soon to get involved.

Bates adds, 'I could not believe it when Colin first told me. Here we were, playing magnificent football and pushing for top spot and the manager would not talk to us about his thoughts on the future.

'We were wanting to look ahead to the next season, way beyond this one. It was not unreasonable. I had an uneasy feeling.'

Gullit was in control of a successful side and had the English game at his feet, yet he was not enthusiastic. Stories started to creep out and rumours began to circulate, but the Dutchman just said, 'There is no problem. I am sure I will sign a new contract.' Bates was not so sure. 'I used to drive home at night wondering why he would not talk terms, indeed not sit down with us at all. I smelt a rat.'

The rat smelt even stronger on Sunday 4 January when

Chelsea, the holders, staged the pick of the third round, a lunchtime kickoff at home to Manchester United. When Bates got the Chelsea teamsheet in the boardroom before the game he feared the worst. No Vialli, and Mark Hughes in midfield. 'My heart dropped,' he said. Chelsea were 5–0 down before Vialli came on to give the score some respectability. 'We only started playing when the side looked the right shape and the right people were in the right position. I have no idea what got into Gullit's head. He must have had a brainstorm. It was the most embarrassing moment of the season.'

The only consolation Chelsea took out of the match was the after-match verdict from United manager Alex Ferguson. He said that he could tell before the kickoff that his players wanted to beat Chelsea. 'They were up for it all right,' he said. 'I could see that. There was definitely a mood in the dressing room of wanting to show Chelsea, to put them in their place. You can usually tell from players, and my side were determined.'

Chelsea should have taken that as a compliment. United had come determined – because they realised that Chelsea's reputation was growing. They realised that Chelsea had started to believe they were the best and they arrived in London to make sure that, by the end of the game, Chelsea would know who exactly were still the big boys.

Bates recalls, 'We can become the Manchester United of the South and even bigger. But at that time the defeat, and Gullit's mucking about in every sense of the word, was a twist I had not expected. I certainly didn't think that we would have to sack him. It was an extraordinary development.

'I had thought that he would sign a new contract and make us even bigger. Why would he want to go to AC Milan or Feyenoord, as had been rumoured, when we could become as big as them? Why would he want to leave, or force us into a position to sack him?

'But sacked he was, in between the Coca-Cola semi-finals with Arsenal. First a 2–1 defeat at Highbury, when Gullit played at the back and showed us that he was not fit enough and struggling to live with the pace of the Premiership. It was sad to see him. He gave away a goal and it was not until the second half, when he switched to midfield, that he looked anything like the dreadlocked master of old.'

His selection and his performance again appalled the Chelsea directors. Mark Hughes' goal got Chelsea out of jail and gave them hope for the second leg, but it did not do enough to save Gullit from becoming the subject of one of the biggest stories of the season. A few days later, Gullit was sacked amid huge controversy. He demanded answers in a press conference and Chelsea gave them to him the same day. His demands were too great and they also believed that he was not fit enough to warrant a playing contract.

Bates now reflects in the glory of cup success under Vialli and points an accusing finger at anyone who dares to suggest that Chelsea were wrong to make the change. 'Even Ruud must admit that we were right,' he says.

'A lot of people took great delight in mouthing off about what we did, why and how. As usual, those people do not use the same space, time or energy to say that we were right.

'They must think that we are idiots. We don't just wake up one morning and say, "Yes, that's a good idea, let's sack the manager."

'We did it because we had to, it was the best decision for this club at that time. We made it as a board of directors and we made it after much consideration.

'Gullit has only himself to blame. He was the manager of a successful side, and a club with huge ambitions. Only he can answer the question why he allowed himself to get into a situation from which, for us, there was no turning back.

'He was asked and asked again to sit down and talk with Colin Hutchinson. If he says that is not true then it is bullshit. We wanted him to stay and there was the offer of a new contract, a realistic contract, but he chose to delay and in the end we had no option.

'He knew how ambitious we were. Hell, you only have to look at what we have achieved over the last few years. We have come a long, long way. He was right in the middle of it but, clearly, he didn't feel part of it. Not enough to talk about the future, anyway. He let it go.

'Chelsea will always be bigger than anything and anyone. It is certainly bigger than me. I have built it up, but it has been a team effort. I always prefer to say that we have done this, we have done that, rather than I. It has been collective, and I am proud of the work we have done and the people who have achieved it.

'No one could believe it when we got rid of Ruud Gullit. He couldn't, nor could the fans, and the people on the outside certainly didn't understand it. Our supporters have great faith. They have seen the team that has been built and they know that we are backing the manager right the way down the line with investment in new stars.

'Gullit knew that. He could still have been in control. He only had to talk, agree to what we wanted, and I am sure there could have been some give and take. He was stubborn, a fool if you like, and he only has himself to blame.

'He can say what he likes. The bottom line is that we had to sack him and now no one can say that Gianluca Vialli is not the right man for the job. He has achieved so much in a short space of time and I have a gut feeling that there is so much more to come.'

Vialli's first game was that massive return against Arsenal in the Coca-Cola Cup on Wednesday 18 February. The atmosphere hung in the air like a twelfth player because of all that had gone on. There was an excess of nervous energy and inside the Chelsea dressing room Vialli gave an emotional speech to his players. It was the most important night of his career because suddenly he had become the manager – he was no longer just Luca. Players looked upon him in a different light. He was the boss, and in those minutes before the kickoff he had to prove it.

Vialli's speech was superb, full of controlled passion, details of how he wanted the side to play plus individual advice. He picked himself. He had to, didn't he? After all that had gone on he simply had to prove to everyone that a lot of time had been wasted. By the time the team left the dressing room the atmosphere was electric – and how Chelsea responded!

They tore into Arsenal with a ferocity that often comes when situations have changed the atmosphere of a club. The players gave everything and charged through to the Wembley final with a 3–1 victory. 'I will never forget the night for as long as I live,' admitted Vialli. 'It was one of the most emotional games I have played in. I cannot thank the players enough.'

It was certainly the turning point of the season, a season that proved so much to Bates, a season that literally had everything. Bates recalls the night like this, 'When I sat down to watch the game, I realised that something special was going to happen. The atmosphere was fantastic.

'It was a game that had you on the edge of your seat throughout, and I was proud of the players. You felt that they were fighting and winning not only for themselves and the club, but for Luca too. He is an immensely popular person and I was delighted for him. It took the pressure off him and us. The bonus was that we had reached another Cup Final, our second inside a year.'

The night clearly took a lot out of the players and they lost the next match, away to Leicester. It was the old inconsistency returning, although on this occasion it could understandably be excused.

The Coca-Cola Cup Final, on Sunday 29 March was, ironically, against Middlesbrough, the side Chelsea had beaten in the FA Cup Final only ten months earlier. Boro had Paul Gascoigne this time, signed from Glasgow Rangers, although manager Bryan Robson decided to keep him on the bench and go with the players who had got Middlesbrough to Wembley again. Vialli kept his own side a secret until just before the kickoff and, interestingly, he did not pick himself. Vialli was not even on the subs' bench and gave the role to Mark Hughes. It was another gesture that increased his popularity in the dressing room.

Chelsea were easy winners and Vialli celebrated long and hard with his players on the pitch. It was another Blue Day for the club and Vialli was a winning manager just five weeks after being given the job. As the song 'Blue Day', which has become Chelsea's signature tune, blared out around Wembley, Bates looked down with satisfaction. 'Another trophy, another step towards what we want to achieve, what we are going to achieve,' he said.

Chelsea continued to frustrate in the Premiership. They were always in touch with the leaders and yet never convincing enough to instil real belief that they could put a run together and win the title. In the end, they lost too many games to deserve the Championship. It was in Europe that they came to life again, proving once more that they were an outstanding cup side, but without the pedigree, for now, to be Champions.

Real Betis from Spain were taken on and dismissed in the quarterfinal and then came the epic semi against Vicenza from Italy. Vialli had warned his squad that to be real Champions you have to be better than the Italians. Chelsea lost the first leg, and they were somewhat fortunate to concede only one goal. It looked all over in the return in London when the Italians scored first. Chelsea needed three goals.

Gustavo Poyet immediately pulled one back and the atmosphere and expectancy grew. Bates says, 'In the directors' lounge at half time, we all thought that if we could get another one quickly then we might do it. I couldn't wait for the second half to begin.'

Nor could Vialli and his little friend, Gianfranco Zola. Vialli produced a superb turn of pace and made a run down the right and the smallest man on the pitch, little Zola, powered his cross in at the far post. It was a thrilling goal, a magnificent header.

The clock ticked, and so did Chelsea hearts, until coach Graham Rix made the crucial decision to send on Hughes. He rattled the defenders immediately, charging into them and generally upsetting them. Then he produced one of the goals of his career. A pass released Hughes into an area down the left of the penalty box. Everyone was expecting a cross until Hughes unleashed a left-footed shot that flew past the goalkeeper and into the bottom corner.

Stamford Bridge erupted and Bates got to his feet in celebration as the Chelsea players engulfed Hughes. It was one of the great moments of a momentous season.

Another final, this time a European one against Stuttgart in

Stockholm on 13 May. Chelsea had already qualified for the UEFA Cup by virtue of their league position but they were hungry for a European trophy, their first since 1971 when they won this same competition against Real Madrid in Athens after a replay. It was as if Chelsea were meant to win. It was not an outstanding performance but the fairy tale was in place when Zola came off the subs' bench to score a spectacular winner and earn the man of the match award. It was an ironic twist for the little Italian, who had lost form and his place in the Italian World Cup squad. Zola could not hide his delight. His huge smile spread across the whole of Sweden and there were wild scenes in the dressing room with the players, the manager and staff, and Bates and his directors all coming together as one.

The on-pitch celebration had been wild. At one stage, all the Chelsea players joined hands and ran the length of the pitch before diving full length, Jurgen Klinsmann-style, in front of a huge bank of Chelsea fans. Bates says, 'You can't make up nights like that, situations that mean so much.

'When this is all over I will have wonderful memories. That night in Stockholm will be just one of them.'

Two trophies in a season, three in a year, a new manager, Vialli winning two cups in a matter of months – you certainly couldn't make that up. For Bates it was the kind of success he had waited for, and he was not going to let anyone rest who doubted his plans.

He now says, 'As I have said many times, this club has been living in the past. For years I listened to crap about the seventies and the team they had then. It does not compare with this one. Let's get that right.

'I don't know why people still look back. The seventies were a disaster for this club. They tried to build that stand and had to sell the players to pay for it. In 1982 it was still a mess, but now I can honestly say that we have got it right.

'People should give us credit. We have won three trophies in a year. And now we want the Championship. At the rate we are progressing we will be European Champions before you know it.

'We have a great team and we are playing great football in a superb new stadium. And we haven't finished yet. I said we would do it and we have.

'I know, we all know, that there can be no rest. After we won in Europe, I got cornered by some fans on the way home. They told me where we went wrong in the Championship. They said that we needed four defenders, a striker, a midfielder . . . they went on and on.

'I can understand that because we have lifted the expectancy level way beyond any of these people's dreams. We have given them success and now they want more. Success is like a drug.

'You taste it, it gets into your body and you want more – that is how I feel. For years and years I strove to get this club where it is today. All those people who tried to stop me, and they know who they are – and yes, I include Matthew Harding in that, he didn't want me to succeed – I hope that somewhere, somehow they can find the time to say to themselves, "Yes, he did what he said he would do."

'One person had the cheek to ask me if I would now retire, suggesting that it was time to go because I had achieved all that I had set out to do. Time to go? They must be joking. This is only just beginning. I will still be here when I am 120 years old. I can never see myself quitting Chelsea.

'What would I do? This has been my life. I love everything about it. I love the fans, the ground, the team – I love it all. I get up in the morning and look forward to going to work.

'And when I swing into the front entrance, there it is, the club we have built. The bricks, the grass, the team . . . the dream.

'And now there are new goals. I set myself new goals and targets all the time. I have to. No day is the same. You cannot look back. You must look forward.

'I will not rest until Chelsea are the Champions of England, Champions of Europe, the best team there is. Only then will I say to myself, "Well done, Ken, that's it. Go home."'

12 The New Chelsea

GIANLUCA VIALLI ALLOWED HIMSELF a sip of champagne on the flight back home from Stockholm. It was a sip of success and a drink to the future all in one.

Behind him his players laughed and joked with their wives and girlfriends as the drink flowed and the conversation grew louder. Then, the directors sat smugly, happy that they had given the job to this millionaire legend from Italy.

The media came next, squashed together, thinking of the stories to write. Like Vialli, they were not thinking of the game any more, it was the follow-ups, the next day that was important to them.

The VIP fans could not control their emotions. Awash with success and booze, they sang all the way home, much to the annoyance of some journalists trying to type and transcribe tapes.

Vialli heard all this going on and pushed it to the back of his mind. He talked with anyone who passed by or sat next to him, but all the time he was planning, working out the next stage of his career as Chelsea manager. He had already told the Chelsea directors that it was his ambition and intention to win the Championship. They had told him yes, they would support him all the way down the line.

By the time Chelsea's chartered flight had reached Heathrow Vialli knew the direction in which he was going. He knew that new players had to be signed. He knew that if Chelsea were going to be Champions of England then the squad, the side sitting behind him, would have to be strengthened. Some of the Chelsea players flying home in celebration would have to go, they would have to be replaced. It is a cruel game, football. You can never relax. There is always the next challenge; there is always a better player to sign.

By the time Vialli was given the job, Danish International Brian Laudrup had already been wooed by former manager Gullit. Talks had progressed and contract details discussed with the Glasgow Rangers player and his business advisors. Gullit had met Laudrup twice and his method of doing transfers was established. He makes contact with the player and asks if he would be interested in joining the club. If it is positive then everything is passed over to the club and Colin Hutchinson, the chief executive. 'I have no interest in financial details or how much the player is earning,' Gullit would say. 'I make the contact and the rest is up to the club. If they reach agreement, fine, if not, we go on to someone else.'

What annoyed Gullit was his discovery that Laudrup had visited London for a lunch with Vialli, Gianfranco Zola and Hutchinson behind his back, before he had been told that he was sacked. Gullit believed, and still does to this day, that Chelsea had gone behind his back. He was furious with Vialli and the incident only widened the gulf between them.

Gullit heard that Vialli had embraced Laudrup and welcomed him as the manager of the club, even though Gullit was still in control. Chelsea deny all charges. 'Totally wrong,' says Hutchinson. 'Vialli was there at my request and never once was he introduced as manager.'

The fact remains however that Vialli, when in control, was asked about the famous Dane and said that he would be delighted to sign the forward, who can play either wide or down the middle. Negotiations were far advanced but Chelsea say they would have pulled out if Vialli had said no, knocking down Gullit's claim that the deal was done by Vialli behind his back.

Laudrup was a free transfer from Rangers and Gullit had worked hard on him under the Bosman ruling. The player is free but the wage demand is high, that is the unwritten law of the Bosman deals. Chelsea already had five players on £1 million a year contracts: Zola, Frank LeBoeuf, Roberto Di Matteo, Vialli and Gullit himself, who was paid up until the end of June when his contract expired.

The Sky television money has been a massive help to all Premiership clubs. Sponsorship deals have grown with the publicity but where do Chelsea get the other monies from? 'Mind your own fucking business,' says Bates.

Chelsea knew that Ajax, the powerful Dutch side, were also interested in Laudrup, whose wife Mette was known to be close to negotiations and could well have the final say in the deal. She was concerned about schools and housing for her family and was bitterly disappointed at the response from Ajax when she visited Holland.

It was then that Chelsea played their trump card, for which they can thank Hutchinson, the man who stays in the background but has nonetheless become a key figure in the running of the club and the signing of players. When the Laudrups visited London as a family, they were met by a chauffeur-driven limo and whisked around the centre and outskirts, looking at schools, houses and areas most suited to Mette Laudrup's demands. Hutchinson knew that if the wife was happy then Chelsea had a good chance of getting their man.

Another masterstroke followed when Hutchinson went to Glasgow for more talks. Before the meeting took place, Hutchinson opened his leather briefcase and pulled out a blue Chelsea shirt bearing the name of the Laudrup's young son, Nikolei. They were impressed, even more impressed when Hutchinson dug deep a second time and came out with another shirt, this time for daughter Rasmine, with her name and age printed on the back.

It is said that Mrs Laudrup was taken by Chelsea there and then, and that it was the moment when the club clinched the signing of Laudrup.

There was still more drama to follow. Rangers believed that they could squeeze a fee out of Chelsea and started to make noises for £7 million. The Bosman deals are conducted between English and foreign clubs and Rangers claimed that, as they were from Britain, a fee was still due. Bates met their request in typical mood. 'They are pissing in the wind,' he said. 'There will be no fee. The player is ours and this is another example of our success in handling the Bosman system. End of story.'

He was right and Laudrup signed for Chelsea and, it is claimed, became the third-best player in the world. 'You would not expect me to get out our file and show you what the Chelsea players earn,' added Bates. 'What I will say is that if you want the best, and if you want to become the English Champions, you have to pay the best.'

Where would Laudrup play? It is known that he favours a central striker's role although Rangers used him more as a flank forward. The signing was met with interest by Chelsea's other attacking players, Mark Hughes, Zola and Tore Andre Flo. There was also Vialli himself. More signings were to follow and again Vialli went for an attacking player, another central striker, when everyone thought he would be hellbent on strengthening his defence. Vialli went back to Italy and chased former international Pierluigi Casiraghi, playing with Lazio and on the fringe of his country's World Cup squad. Vialli made contact with his friend, who told him that he wanted to play in English football and would love to come to London and Chelsea. Enter Hutchinson again.

He made a flying visit to Rome and talked with Lazio officials. Hutchinson was told that negotiations would have to stay on hold until after Lazio's UEFA Cup commitments. The fee for Casiraghi was £5.4 million and the salary was another £1 million a year.

Hutchinson was not put off. He kept in touch with the Italian club and the moment their UEFA Cup run was over, he was on another plane to complete the deal. It was a three-year contract for the 29-year-old star. Casiraghi was signed to add to Chelsea's extraordinary array of attacking talent. Something or someone had to go, surely? The Italian, said Vialli, would be suited to the English game because of his robust, European style. Chelsea were now reaching the point when they could not possibly keep everyone happy, especially Hughes who in July made a £650,000 move to Southampton.

There is no question that the bigger the name, the easier it is to attract the world stars. If a player receives a call from a legend like Vialli then he is going to be interested. It was the same with Gullit. Arsene Wenger has a similar respect at Arsenal. The competition to attract the array of talent on offer in Europe is fierce.

Wenger is concerned at where it will end. He says that before Bosman a handful of clubs like Barcelona, Real Madrid, Inter and AC Milan, Manchester United and one or two others had the pick of the crop because they were the clubs with the big money, generated by their large crowds. European television money and the Bosman ruling have opened up a huge network. Wenger says, 'There are now about sixty clubs all screaming out for the players. The price goes up with the demand. Players are demanding, and getting, huge amounts of money.'

It did not put off Chelsea. Vialli and Hutchinson were soon back on a plane, this time aiming for Spain, to target Barcelona's experienced fullback Albert Ferrer. Chelsea have needed strengthening and Vialli quickly and secretly did a £2.2 million deal for the 28-year-old, right-sided player. Another three-year contract and another near £1 millon a year agreement.

Two days later came perhaps the biggest and best signing of Chelsea's summer. Hutchinson was off on his travels once more, this time to France's World Cup training camp where they swooped for French international Marcel Desailly.

This, perhaps, was the signing that signalled Chelsea's real intention to win the Championship in 1998/99. Desailly is top class, world class, and a number of clubs were chasing him hard. Vialli's initial contact and Hutchinson's persistence made sure that they got their man.

Desailly, 28, who won big trophies with Milan, including the Champions' League and Serie A, can play either in midfield or as a central defender. 'At my age I have to have new ambition and Chelsea have provided that,' he says.

'In my five years with Milan I won three championships and now I want to win one again in another country. Chelsea have convinced me of their ambition, their progress, and I want to help them become the best.

'Gianluca Vialli has told me of his own ambitions, his own plans and how and where he wants me to play. I will play either as a defender or in midfield, I do not mind. It is a very important move for me and I have chosen England because football there is growing and becoming bigger and better all the time.

'I saw Chelsea win the Cup Winners' Cup and I am told that their two trophies are just the start. I am happy to be here at the start of their rise to become the Champions of Europe.' If Chelsea do win the Championship this season then Desailly's £4.6 million fee and his £35,000 a week, four-year contract will be a good investment.

The signing took Vialli's spending to £7 million in two days and £12 million in two weeks, which was on top of the huge wages bill. You have to hand it to them, however, as once again they acted quickly, doing their business soon after the end of the season and before any of their rivals knew what was happening. Bates says, 'We never shout about our transfer dealings, never talk about who we would like to sign and never confirm a signing until it has been signed, sealed and delivered.'

The competition for places at Chelsea is now extraordinary. Vialli had a complete team playing in the French World Cup: Ed De Goey (Holland), Albert Ferrer (Spain), Frank Sinclair (Jamaica), Frank LeBoeuf (France), Celestine Babayaro (Nigeria), Dan Petrescu (Romania), Marcel Desailly (France), Roberto Di Matteo (Italy), Graeme Le Saux (England), Tore Andre Flo (Norway) and Brian Laudrup (Denmark).

It is an expensive and, on paper, superb array of talent and when you add Dennis Wise, Pierluigi Casiraghi, Michael Duberry, Eddie Newton, Gustavo Poyet, Vialli, Gianfranco Zola and a young player like Jody Morris to that list, it means the competition for places is frightening. How Vialli is going to keep them all happy I have no idea.

It is going to be a huge test of his man-management skills.

Vialli is very popular in the dressing room and he will need to be if he is to juggle that array of talent around and make sure they are all committed mentally. For instance, if Casiraghi and Zola start up front and Chelsea have a successful start to the season, how does he keep Flo, Norway's World Cup centre forward and one of the best young strikers in Europe, happy. It is a massive problem.

Vialli has told his players that this is a squad situation and that Chelsea, like England in the World Cup, will be run on a system – they are all in it together. But I foresee problems.

It is also a big problem for the young players who are progressing through the ranks, like Morris. His chances are going to be very limited this season and he will have to make a decision about his career, whether to stay at Chelsea and be a reserve, even if he is learning from the world-class players around him, or go elsewhere.

Young Danny Granville made his own decision in June 1998 when he decided that he had to move on to develop his career. Leeds made a £1.6 million offer and Chelsea accepted it after negotiation. Granville said, 'When I looked at the players being signed by the club, and the number of big names competing for places, I knew I had to move on. I had no alternative. I had tasted first-team football and did not want to spend a season, or maybe two, playing the odd game. It would have been no good for my development.'

This fee, for a player snapped up for just £200,000 from Cambridge, represents a huge profit by Chelsea – good business when you can get it. But is it? Will Chelsea regret their decision in the long term?

There are not many left-sided players, top-class left-footed players, in the country and Granville is rated highly by professionals throughout the game. However, the exit was inevitable because at Chelsea something has to give when so many players are pushing for eleven positions. I suspect that in the end it will be George Graham, the manager of Leeds, who will celebrate the best deal.

At best, he can develop Granville into one of the best wing backs in the country in the Leeds side he believes will one day win the title. At worst he will be able to sell him on in a few seasons' time at another massive profit. The irony will be if Granville replaces Graeme Le Saux, the first choice at Chelsea, in the England side.

The concern over the development of young players is a situation that the whole of English football faces. There are those, like England coach Glenn Hoddle, who fear that in ten years there will be no homegrown talent left. Gordon Taylor, the chief executive of the PFA, says that the European player in English football is fine, just as long as he is first class and a first choice. Taylor argues that clubs are going into Europe to get the cheap players, thus lowering the standard of the game here.

That cannot be levelled at Chelsea. Their summer signings were all internationals, all world-class players and simply represented their aim to be the best.

It was the signing of Desailly that was the most significant, and the one that pleased the club the most. To get this great French international at his peak represented a huge break-through for them. Desailly drove a hard bargain and his contract demands were high. The transfer fee and his four-year contract make it the biggest investment by this famous West London club in years.

Bates says, 'When we offered Vialli the job, we talked of the future and he asked about our commitment to bringing world-class players to Stamford Bridge. Ever since Hoddle was the manager we have stuck with the attitude that if the manager wants a player, we try and get him. And we usually do.

'These are exciting times. Every season we have improved, every season we have strengthened the squad and every season we have shown our commitment to becoming the best.'

At the start of every season, Chelsea do their sums carefully and their gate receipts pay for the wages. Last season, 1997/98, it was only the home tie with Sheffield Wednesday that did not sell out, and that followed an important European week.

The money from television and sponsorship is the jam, and that jam was spread thickly in the summer of 1998 with four top-class players all captured before the World Cup. That was another target for Colin Hutchinson – he was determined to strike and get his men quickly because he knew reputations and values would rise once France 98 got under way.

It was good business, no doubt, but the pressure is now on Chelsea to win something and get an adequate return on the money that has been spent. With that array of talent it will be staggering if they do not capture at least one trophy. We know they can win cups, now they want the biggest of all. The League. To be the Champions.

Vialli believes he has built the squad to do it. Bates hopes so. Oh, how he hopes so.

13 My Best Chelsea Team

THE QUESTION WAS SIMPLE ENOUGH and it brought an instant answer from Ken Bates. What is the best Chelsea side there has been in your sixteen years of control – the one that has given you most pleasure? 'That's easy,' he said. 'The current one.'

There was not a moment's hesitation. Unusual, perhaps, considering the number of players Bates has seen from his chairman's seat in the front row of the directors' box – Glenn Hoddle, Kerry Dixon, David Speedie, Pat Nevin, the list is endless . . . Ruud Gullit even. 'Definitely this one,' said Bates. 'Why? That's easy too,' he added. 'Because it is a winning team.'

That is easy to understand. Bates has always viewed himself as a winner. From the day he walked into Stamford Bridge to the first game of the 1998/99 season, away to Coventry – a repeat of the previous season – Bates has wanted only one thing. To be the best.

'To be the best there can only be one answer,' he adds. 'To have the best team. A winning team. There have been some good memories down the years, some good players and some good teams. This is a great team and it is going to get even better. How can I choose another side when this current one makes me excited, gives the expectancy of winning, wins two Cup Finals in a season, three in a year?'

The construction of the side was started by Hoddle, carried on by Gullit and extended by Gianluca Vialli. For me, they are still a team that can beat anyone in the country, in Europe for that matter, but their consistency is still questionable when it comes to winning the Championship, the biggest prize of all and the one that Bates and Vialli want most of all.

In goal, Chelsea's first choice is Ed De Goey, the tall Dutchman signed by Gullit. He is a marvellous shot stopper and yet is prone to making crucial mistakes. Towards the end of the 1997/98 season, Vialli used De Goey and Russian international Dimitri Kharine in alternate matches in the Premiership while he made up his mind which player would be his first choice. It was not a decision that pleased De Goey, even if he did play in the Coca-Cola Cup Final and Cup Winners' Cup Final victories. Neither goalkeeper would sit on the bench as cover for the other because the rivalry is too great.

They say that to win the Championship in England you must have a great goalscorer and a great goalkeeper. Chelsea do not have a great keeper amongst the four on their books. The other two are Kevin Hitchcock, a marvellous servant of the club and a good team man, and Frode Grodas, Norway's captain in the World Cup, again signed by Gullit. He spent the end of the season on loan at Spurs as cover to Ian Walker.

It is the defence that continually worries critics and fans – and directors if they are honest. You are never surprised when Chelsea concede a goal, or lose a game that you feel should provide a comfortable win. It has happened too many times. French international Frank LeBoeuf is a wonderful player, but not a great defender. He often struggles in a flat back four and is far more comfortable as the spare defender in a sweeper system.

The 1998/99 season is a big one for Michael Duberry. He returned from serious injury soon after the start of last season and has not, as yet, completely returned to the form that he showed before. His potential is enormous and he must prove that he can develop as an international defender.

At fullback, Graeme Le Saux is quality, although his attacking game is far superior to his defensive play. Under pressure and up against an out and out winger he can be vulnerable; going forward there is not a better 'wing back' in the country. He is a regular with England and he had an outstanding World Cup.

On the right, Frank Sinclair has pace and is good in the air but his distribution, for a player who gets a lot of the ball, is not good enough. A good Premiership defender, but not a great one. Not good enough for a Championship-winning side, and that is what Chelsea want to be in 1998/99.

Steve Clarke has seen it, done it, and now won it at Chelsea. He says, 'I got fed up with people talking to me about Osgood, Hudson and the best side Chelsea had. Our FA Cup Final victory in 1997 put an end to that and we have since gone from strength to strength.

'I am pleased for the chairman because we are now giving him what he always wanted.' Clarke played in Chelsea's cup-winning sides but may have to be content with a bit-part in the new season as fresh arrivals, younger legs, take over.

In midfield, Chelsea have outstanding options of real quality. Captain Dennis Wise has improved beyond recognition in recent seasons. His temperament will let him down at times and he has a fierce tackle for a little fella, often illegal, but his passing makes him one of the best midfield players in the country. His range, short and long, is superb. When Wise plays well, so do Chelsea.

Dan Petrescu was one of Hoddle's best signings. Signed from Sheffield Wednesday after a recommendation from his friend Chris Waddle, Petrescu was used as a wing back in Hoddle's favoured three-five-two formation. He has now been pushed forward and his passing and awareness are invaluable, although when the going gets tough Petrescu can go missing.

Gullit and Vialli have both been criticised for signing players from Italy who are too old or over the hill. Not so with Roberto Di Matteo. He was captured at the age of 26 and has signed a new contract with the club. The Italians would like to have him back and Chelsea turned down two offers in the summer of 1998. His strength from box to box is outstanding and his passing is impressive. He will go down in the history books for his magnificent goal in the opening seconds of the 1997 FA Cup Final.

Gustavo Poyet is one of those players who the fans love to love. Chelsea supporters responded to this Uruguay international straight away because of his work rate, flair and his ability to float unnoticed into the box to score important goals. He suffered a terrible injury at the start of the 1997/98 season but recovered to play a key role in the European success.

Eddie Newton will never forget his match-clinching goal in the FA Cup Final victory over Middlesbrough in 1997. 'It was the greatest moment of my life,' he says. Newton, liked by Gullit in the role of midfield anchorman, has recovered from a broken leg to be a vital part of Chelsea's success. He has been at the club for years and has seen many changes. The biggest, the arrival of all the foreign stars, may frustrate him. He was left out of the Cup Winners' Cup Final because of the return to fitness of Poyet. He may be on the outside looking in this season.

Gianfranco Zola is loved by everyone at Chelsea. Bates says, 'He is one of the nicest footballers, no, people, I have ever met. He always has a smile on his face. He loves Chelsea and we love him.' In his first season, Zola won the coveted Football Writers' Footballer of the Year award and thrilled Stamford Bridge with his skills, pace, control and ability to produce the unexpected. It broke his heart when, last season, his form dropped and he was axed from Italy's World Cup squad. But he will never forget one of the great moments of his career, coming off the bench to score the winning goal in the Cup Winners' Cup Final. 'It was, how do you say in England, magic,' smiled Zola. The little Italian and Bates were seen embracing shortly after the wonderful on-pitch celebrations.

Tore Andre Flo was signed for peanuts, about £500,000, and has proved marvellous business. This gangling Norwegian forward has great skill for a tall man; his control is close and he has the ability to score goals, particularly in the air – very impressive. Chelsea's problem is going to be keeping him happy. His reputation is growing and he wants to play in every game. With the competition for places getting fiercer, Vialli could have a problem here.

Another favourite with the fans is Mark Hughes. When his

agent, Dennis Roach, offered Hughes to Hoddle, Chelsea could not have believed they would be signing such a winner. Many thought that Hughes was past his best. Not so. He responded in London and proved that United had made a terrible mistake, so big was the mistake that United tried to buy him back after one season.

Hughes is loved because he plays every game as if his life depends on it. His character changes once he crosses the white line. He changes from a subdued, quiet, laid back man into a battle-hardened forward who does not know the meaning of the word defeat. He upsets defenders and he is booked more than he should be, but he is worth his weight in gold to the club. No one at Chelsea will ever forget his winning goal in the Cup Winners' Cup semi-final second leg at Stamford Bridge. He will, I'm sure be missed by each and every Chelsea fan.

Another favourite with the Stamford Bridge faithful is Gianluca Vialli. His popularity grew long before he was made manager. They had heard about Vialli for years and when he arrived they could only marvel at his skills, his famous bald head and beard – and his goals.

Not once did they drop their hero worship when Gullit was treating him badly, leaving him out and not playing him for weeks. When he warmed up as sub they screamed their delight and often demanded his arrival from the bench.

He was the obvious replacement for Gullit, just as the Dutchman had been for Glenn Hoddle. Vialli gave them two trophies in his first few weeks as manager, at the end of the 1997/98 season. Bates says, 'His first game in charge was the Coca-Cola Cup semi-final against Arsenal. I felt for him because we had sacked Gullit and the pressure was on Luca. When we won so wonderfully on one of the great nights at Stamford Bridge, I went into the dressing room to hug him. It was a chairman and manager moment, hard to explain but vital in a relationship.'

Vialli's playing contract runs out at the end of the new season and I suspect his appearances will get fewer and fewer. In his mind he is now a manager more than a player, and he desperately wants the Championship. He has always been a champion in Italy. Now he wants to be the king of London football.

Other players have given Bates satisfaction and make his best-team selection easier. Players like Danny Granville, a bargain signing from Cambridge; Andy Myers, home grown and who can play at the centre of the defence, at left back or in midfield; Babayaro, the Nigerian so highly rated by the club; Lambourde, the Frenchman who has yet to show Chelsea his true pedigree; Jody Morris, the small midfield star who is tipped for a big future but whose progress may be stifled by the new arrivals; and Mark Nicholls, another local boy who has dropped into the side on many occasions.

Bates looks at the squad with real satisfaction. He says, 'How could I select another side, other players, when this one has won things?

'When we won the Cup Winners' Cup in Stockholm and I sat in their directors' box and watched the players celebrate in style, I could think of only one thing. It was thank you. I don't know really to whom. Someone up there, the people who have supported me, me if you like, but here it all was coming together in front of my eyes.

'All the hard work, the fights, the anguish, the pain, the tears, the heartache, the smiles, the black days, the good ones – they were all worthwhile. Here was a winning Chelsea side. A Chelsea side with style, a team to give pleasure and bring the club success. It has taken sixteen years but, my God, it has been worth it.'

While on holiday in Italy in the summer of 1998, Bates and Suzannah saw a familiar figure while they sat on their yacht. The man was walking along the quayside and talking into a mobile phone. He was just about to board his own yacht when Suzannah said to Bates, 'You know who that is, don't you?' It was Vialli.

At the top of his voice, Bates shouted, 'Gianluca Vialli!' The meeting had not been planned but the manager and his chairman spent the next few hours together. They chatted about a lot of things – Italy, wine, food, restaurants, football, Chelsea. They discussed the new signings and the ones Vialli still wanted to make.

They thought about the new season and they chatted about the World Cup. 'He had shaved off his beard, which is probably why I didn't recognise him at first,' said Bates. 'It was an enjoyable time. I thanked him for what he had done in such a short time.'

Who knows? If Bates is asked the same question – name your best and most enjoyable Chelsea side – in the summer of 1999, he may change his mind and say it is the current team, the one that Vialli built for the 1998/99 season. 'I hope I can say that the Premiership Champions are the best Chelsea side of all time,' adds the chairman. 'It is what I have always wanted.'